smart

DISCIPLINE®

smart

DISCIPLINE®

Fast, Lasting Solutions for Your Peace
of Mind and Your Child's Self-Esteem

LARRY J. KOENIG, PH.D.

HarperResource
An Imprint of HarperCollins*Publishers*

Letters from parents and responses written by Larry J. Koenig, Ph.D., in chapter 15 first appeared in the column titled "Family Matters" in the *Southeast News*. Reprinted by permission of *Southeast News*.

Smart Discipline® is a registered trademark of Larry J. Koenig.

HarperCollins books may be purchased for educational, business, or sales promotional use. For information please write to: Special Markets Department, HarperCollins Publishers Inc., 10 East 53rd Street, New York, New York 10022.

FIRST EDITION

DESIGNED BY MARY AUSTIN SPEAKER

Library of Congress Cataloging-in-Publication has been applied for.

ISBN 0-06-621239-1

02   03   04   05   06   QW   10   9   8   7   6   5   4   3   2

To Nydia

CONTENTS

ACKNOWLEDGMENTS

Acknowledgment pages have always been a curiosity to me. They seem like the many credits that roll at the end of a movie. I always marvel at how many names are listed. Then I wonder out loud to my wife, Nydia, "Why in the world does it take so many people to make a movie?" She, like me, is baffled.

The mystery has now been solved for me—at least the one about why authors thank so many people. A book is a major undertaking. I can trace the beginning concepts for this book back fifteen years. During this time, there have been lots of people, both adults and children, who have helped and influenced me. Without them, this book would still be but a dream.

In this book, I talk about how important it is to instill positive beliefs in children and to help them identify and come to believe in their God-given talents. My parents, Harold J. and Margaret E. Koenig, did this for me. They chose to seek out the good in me even when I was acting the opposite. When a mysterious and well-hidden congenital defect threatened to take my life, they resolutely pushed the doctors to take another look and yet another look until the problem was identified and the solution enacted. Throughout the turmoil that life has brought to me as an adult, they have always been there for me—lovingly and unconditionally. I wish all children could have parents like them!

To my children, Saul, Sally, Andrea, Jennifer, and Catherine, I want to say thank you for putting up with me—my hours of writing, my silliness, and my adventures in life. I am so very proud of each of you.

Life is difficult, but you all have accomplished much despite the obstacles and challenges thrown your way. The examples from your early years that ended up in the book will serve to help many—and I thank you for them.

Professionally, I would like to express my appreciation to the following. To Summer Doucet, thanks for the great work on the first edits of the book. Thanks to Dr. Mark Viator for being a champion of Smart Discipline and steadfast friend. To friend and fellow author Max Davis, I say thanks with all of my heart. Without your guidance and freely given advice, this book would not exist. Thanks to Rick Frishman of Planned Television Arts (PTA) for his expert help in developing the proposal for the book. To Judy Johnson, I want to say thank you so very much. It was your brilliant design work that got me noticed from coast to coast.

To the thousands of parents and children who have used and are using Smart Discipline throughout the world, I say thank you and good luck. Many of you have written to me over the years. I have always appreciated your thank-you notes and especially am grateful for the questions and suggestions that have helped refine Smart Discipline.

To the many psychologists and other mental health professionals who have validated Smart Discipline by teaching it to your patients and using it with your own children, I am and will remain grateful. To my network of presenters who teach the Smart Discipline seminars throughout North America, I owe a major debt of gratitude. Many of you have become friends and avid supporters of Smart Discipline over the years. Because of you, thousands of families are helped each year. Thank you for spreading the work and skillfully helping so many.

To Dr. Stephen Allen, I want to say a special thank-you. You were the very first to spread the word about Smart Discipline in a major way. Your friendship, support, and ideas have helped me to keep going more than you will ever know.

To Toni Sciarra, my editor at HarperCollins, I send my kudos. Having never had a book edited by a senior editor at a major publishing house, I was so very afraid that you were going to send my manuscript back with a note that read, "What high school did you graduate from, if any?" Instead of criticizing, you were incredibly kind and wonderfully skillful in "bringing out the best in me" as a writer.

I have saved my last thank-you for my wife, Nydia. You are the "wow" of my life. Without your loving support and enthusiastic belief in me, I wouldn't be getting to tell the world right now how much I love you. I wish everyone could be married to someone like you. It would be a kinder, gentler, and more civil world!

PART ONE

The Smart Discipline System

1

Getting Started
with Smart Discipline

Stop your children's fighting and bickering? Get your kids to do what you ask the first time—without having to yell and scream at them? You bet. These are both doable. And what a wonderful difference it will make when your children are self-motivated to follow the rules at home and at school.

Smart Discipline is used by thousands of parents who have wearied of the daily battles with their children. These parents now know that parenting can be a great joy. They have found out firsthand that parents and children can live together peacefully—and that children can learn to get along without being miserably difficult.

Wouldn't it be nice if you could get your children to

- stop their fighting and bickering.
- stop their whining.
- stop interrupting you on the phone.
- do their homework—on time and without hassles.
- go to bed on time—and stay there!
- get up and ready for school on time—without your having to nag.
- follow the rules without being warned dozens of times.
- do their chores—before you ask them.
- be respectful—to you and to their siblings.
- pick up their rooms.
- behave at school.

Each of these things is possible. Hundreds of psychologists and family therapists in the United States and Canada teach Smart Discipline in their practices. Some even require the families who are their clients to use the system. When I ask them why, they tell me simply, "Because it works." They explain that while there is lots of good parenting information out there, Smart Discipline is the one system that is both easy to use and remarkably effective.

Here's how I know they aren't just paying me lip service. These same psychologists go on to say how they use Smart Discipline with their own children. One recently related to me how his six-year-old son told him at bedtime, "I could have had my snack if I would have chosen to pick up my room on time. Tomorrow night I think I will just go ahead and do it early." This father/psychologist said to me, "I couldn't have taught my son this. This is a lesson Smart Discipline taught him."

My wife, Nydia, and I know firsthand what he meant. We developed Smart Discipline over several years in our own family. We, too, wanted peace in our house. The bickering, screaming, arguing, bad attitudes, and intolerable behavior had reached a crescendo. Too often we were going to bed frazzled. The next day we would resolve to do better, only to start the day with jangled nerves just trying to get everyone off to school and work.

This is not to say that our children were bad. They were not. But they had developed some pretty maladaptive ways of getting what they wanted. Fortunately, we were able to teach them more civil and peaceful behavioral choices. To do so, we realized we had to come up with a method that would fit into our busy lifestyles, would work for both of us, and was something we could be consistent in using.

The Smart Discipline System was the result. Nydia and I were stunned that our children's behavior and attitudes changed in a matter of several days. Rules ignored before were now being followed without complaint. Schoolwork was being done and handed in on time. One of our children who used to bring bad behavior reports home from teachers started to bring home notes extolling her virtues as a good student. Best of all, we stopped the yelling and screaming that we hated so much.

Both professionals and other parents now get passionate about Smart Discipline. Over three thousand Smart Discipline seminars are planned each year by schools, hospitals, churches, civic groups, and employers. They are the most well-attended parenting seminars in

America. The participants consistently report the same results that Nydia and I experienced with our children.

It is my hope that you, too, will find Smart Discipline to be of great benefit in your family. First, like thousands of other parents, you should find behavior and attitudes to improve rather quickly—within a week or two. Second, as you use the ideas in this book, your children's beliefs about themselves should strengthen. This is a good thing. I firmly believe that children who have positive beliefs about themselves not only do better in school and in life, but are much better behaved while they are growing up.

There is one last major benefit to Smart Discipline. You will strengthen your relationships with your children. The reason this is so very important is that there are millions of teenagers today who have lousy relationships with their parents. This is tragic. Many mothers and fathers have their hearts broken over their children's defiance of them. This is totally avoidable.

Smart Discipline gives parents an effective way to discipline while building and strengthening their bond with their children. You will find that it is perfectly reasonable to be able to inspire good behavior and even to punish bad behavior without destroying your relationship with your children. When you can inspire both cooperation and love at the same time, you have it made as a parent. It is my goal to show you how to do precisely that.

Sounds almost too good to be true, doesn't it? But if you are like most parents dealing with the same old problems day after day, part of you is likely saying, "Oh, man! I sure hope this works. If I could get my children to behave like normal human beings, this book would be worth its weight in gold!"

Having children who willingly and respectfully obey their parents is a wonderful thing. It is even better, though, to have children who have both healthy self-esteem and self-confidence.

The good thing about having children who feel good about themselves is that they tend to be very well behaved. The higher a child's self-esteem, the more well behaved she will be. Sure, there may be periods of misbehavior even in a child with healthy self-esteem, but they will likely not be severe or long-lived.

Instilling self-esteem in your children is an integral part of the

Smart Discipline program. Subsequent to learning the discipline system, you will learn

- how beliefs, both positive and negative, are formed.
- why beliefs are so powerful.
- the three-step process to instill powerful and positive beliefs in your children.
- how to turn negative beliefs into positive ones.

Besides dramatically improving behavior, there are other advantages to helping children grow up with positive beliefs. Children who grow up feeling good about themselves also tend to love their parents dearly. After all, these are the very people who took the time, effort, and love to instill that self-esteem. Perhaps just as important, self-confident children are resistant to negative peer pressure. Because they feel good about themselves, they don't need to "go along" with the others in order to get approval. Instead, they are much more likely to assess the situation and act according to the values they grew up with.

When it comes to discipline, prevention is the key. The best way to handle a discipline problem is to prevent it from happening in the first place. That's what the Smart Discipline System is all about.

HOW THIS BOOK IS ORGANIZED

This book is organized into four parts:

Part One: The Smart Discipline System
In part 1 you will learn the five-step Smart Discipline System. Everything you need to implement the system with your family is included. Immediately after going through this section, you should be able to get started using the system with your children.

In part 1, the system is laid out step by step. You will learn

- how to choose the rules appropriate for your children.
- how to write the rules so they will make sense and be age-appropriate.

- why it is necessary for children to know in advance the consequences for breaking the rules.
- how to select age-appropriate consequences.
- how to set up a Smart Discipline chart.
- how to explain the system to your children in a short family meeting.
- how to use Smart Discipline to get your children to behave at home.
- how to use Smart Discipline to get your children to behave at school.
- how to use Smart Discipline if your child has ADD (attention deficit disorder) or ADHD (attention deficit disorder with hyperactivity).

The hallmarks of the Smart Discipline System are ease of use and effectiveness. You will be able to put the system in place within an hour. And many of you will find that even your children, after some initial balking and complaining, will come to prefer the structure and predictability the Smart Discipline System provides.

Part Two: Bringing Out the Best in Your Children
This section covers how children develop beliefs about themselves—both positive and negative. By using the belief-building techniques I describe, you will also enhance their desire to behave better by bringing out the best in them. A happy by-product of doing so will be a more loving parent/child relationship.

Next you will learn about centers of brilliance. One of the most popular themes I cover with parents is how to help children identify, come to believe in, and develop their inborn, God-given talents. Every child is born with at least three talents. The ones who come to know what their talents are tend to develop a very positive vision for their future. Then they make decisions today based on that vision. These decisions tend to be very good decisions.

Everything you need to identify your children's talents is in this section. Like other parents who have used the Smart Discipline System, you will find that one of the best things you will ever do for your children is to help them to know and to believe in their talents and abilities.

One reason why it is critical for children to know about their talents is that it helps them visualize and to make good, solid decisions about their futures. Children who have no vision of their futures tend to make decisions based on what their friends are doing and on what feels good at the moment.

In essence, children who are aware of their talents are happier, more well-adjusted and better behaved than children who have no idea what their talents are. This is reason enough to take the time and effort to make sure your children come to know and believe in their innate abilities. Even more reason is found in knowing that doing so will provide your children with a solid foundation that will lead to an increased chance for success and happiness.

Part Three: Smart Discipline
Solutions to Homework and School Problems

Even smart, normally well-behaved children can experience or exhibit trouble in these areas from time to time. In some homes, homework hassles are a part of daily living.

In this part of the book, you will learn how to use the Smart Discipline System to get your children to abide by the rules at school. You will also learn the three basic homework rules I suggest that will both prevent and solve almost all your homework woes. In the last chapter of this section, the fifteen most common homework problems are discussed, with step-by-step solutions for each.

Part Four: Parenting Mistakes to
Avoid and Common Parenting Concerns

All parents want their children to grow up to be happy and successful. I am convinced that all parental decisions are rooted in this intention. Being human, though, parents make mistakes. Most are inconsequential. Others can be devastating. In one chapter in part 4, you will find what I consider to be the seven most common mistakes parents make—and what to do instead. Avoid these mistakes and you will save both you and your children a lot of grief.

The last chapter of the book is composed of the typical questions I have received from parents in my travels and speaking engagements in over eight hundred cities throughout the United States. This Q&A chapter serves two purposes. As a parent, you will likely be able to identify with some of the questions and find some of the suggestions very helpful with your own children. Second, you will also get a sense that you are not alone in your struggles to raise your children.

Should you have a question that is not covered in this section, feel free to e-mail me at larry@smartdiscipline.com or visit our Web site: www.smartdiscipline.com.

Just as life can be very difficult, so can parenting. Leave a car dealership with a new car and you get a three-hundred-page instruction manual. Leave a hospital with a baby and you get coupons for some free diapers. Fortunately, though, there is lots of good information available to assist parents. It is my hope that in this book you will find just the help you need to raise happy and successful children.

Step 1:

Identifying Misbehaviors in Need of Change

Many parents these days seek out a psychologist or other mental health professional for help with their children's misbehavior. When they do so, they are asked first to identify in concrete terms the behaviors that they want their children to change. This isn't always an easy task. Parents usually say things like the following:

- "He gets up in the morning and finds every way he can to irritate me. I can't get him to stop. He's driving me crazy!"
- "She won't get up in the morning. When she finally does, it's one hassle after another until she goes to bed at night, which is also a hassle."
- "He won't do anything I say until I scream at him!"
- "I don't know what irritates me more: her bad attitude or her disrespectful language."

I'm sure you can hear the frustration in these statements. It sounds as if these children have major behavior problems. But that's not the case. Usually these are just normal children who have gotten into the habit of getting what they want through some less-than-desirable behavior patterns.

The good news is that you can teach your children how to meet their needs in ways other than those that drive you nuts. The first step is to identify the specific behaviors that you want your children to change. Until you do this, you will be relegated to that large group of parents who remain perennially frustrated with their children's misbehavior.

Once you have identified the behaviors in need of change, you will have the "handle" you need to start motivating your children to use more appropriate behaviors to get what they want.

Typically, our kids are not out there doing awful, terrible, horrible things. No, theirs are more common, everyday misbehaviors. But when these behaviors are repeated over and over again—such as not cleaning their rooms or leaving dirty dishes around the house—they tend to infuriate parents. Don't you hate it when they put those two misbehaviors together? I mean, you move a pile of dirty clothes, only to find that glass you've been looking for over the past month. It's still full of milk; it's just solid milk now.

Negative attitude, talking back, being sassy, not getting up on time, and it wouldn't occur to them to go to bed on time, either, would it?

When one of our daughters went off to Louisiana State University, she moved into the college dormitory, fifteen miles away from home. We were very happy with this situation—at least until she called home eight days later and said, "Dad, I've got to go to the doctor right away."

I replied, "What's the problem? It sounds serious."

"I don't know, Dad, I'm tired all the time. I can't seem to get up for classes in the morning. I fall asleep in half the classes I do get to. I just think I'd better go to the doctor, Dad."

Suspicious, I asked, "Darlin', what time do you go to bed at night?"

Without skipping a beat, she says, "I don't know, Dad. The same time everybody else does—two or three."

"Yeah," I said, "that requires a doctor all right—but a different kind of doctor."

The list of parents' complaints also commonly includes things like not putting toys away, lying, bad manners, and watching too much TV. The average American child today watches thirty-five hours of television per week. By the age of eighteen the average American child today has watched thirty-six thousand hours of television! Definitely too much TV, don't you think?

Other misbehaviors commonly on people's lists include always has an excuse, complains about anything and everything, ignores us, doesn't put things away, borrows things without asking (I call it stealing, but my wife won't let me call it that), doesn't do homework till the last minute, and fights with brothers and sisters. These are just common everyday misbehaviors, but as a parent you know exactly how they tend to drive you up the wall when they're repeated over and over again.

To get you started, here is a checklist to use. Simply check off the behaviors that bother you the most. If you are married, you may want to record your answers on a separate sheet of paper and have your spouse do the same. This way you can see which of the behaviors are bugging both of you the most. These may be the ones you'll want to tackle first. More about this later, but for now go ahead and check off the misbehaviors that commonly occur on a daily basis. If a behavior that bothers you is not listed, enter it at the end of the list in one of the blanks called "other."

STEP ONE IDENTIFYING MISBEHAVIORS

_____ 1. Won't clean room

_____ 2. Whines

_____ 3. Leaves dirty dishes around

_____ 4. Won't obey the first time asked

_____ 5. Leaves toys out

_____ 6. Is defiant

_____ 7. Skips school

_____ 8. Behaves badly at school

_____ 9. Has bad manners

_____ 10. Too much TV

_____ 11. Negative attitude

_____ 12. Talks back

_____ 13. Doesn't get up on time

_____ 14. Won't go to bed on time

_____ 15. Comes home late

_____ 16. Interrupts

_____ 17. Swears, uses foul language

_____ 18. Always has an excuse; denies misbehavior

_____ 19. Constantly complains

_____ 20. Ignores you

_____ 21. Uses disrespectful body language

_____ 22. Is forgetful

_____ 23. Cries easily

_____ 24. Doesn't put things away

_____ 25. Borrows things without asking

_____ 26. Has temper tantrums

_____ 27. Refuses to help

_____ 28. Doesn't pick up after self

_____ 29. Doesn't finish projects

_____ 30. Doesn't keep commitments

_____ 31. Is addicted to video games

_____ 32. Misbehaves in car

_____ 33. Misbehaves while shopping

_____ 34. Misbehaves in restaurants

_____ 35. Hits, kicks, or bites

_____ 36. Engages in name-calling

_____ 37. Bullies others

_____ 38. Is rude to others

_____ 39. Has a sarcastic attitude

_____ 40. Throws things

_____ 41. Talks on phone too much

_____ 42. Leaves the house without permission

_____ 43. Procrastinates on homework

_____ 44. Refuses to do homework

_____ 45. Roughhouses too much

_____ 46. Dresses sloppily

_____ 47. Fights/bickers constantly with siblings

_____ 48. Other _____

_____ 49. Other _____

_____ 50. Other _____

Once you have checked the behaviors that are irritating you most, make a separate list of the behaviors that you want each of your children to change. For children ages three through eight, limit the list to no more than five misbehaviors. For children age nine or older, limit the list to no more than ten items. If your child has ADD or ADHD, regardless of age, start out with only one or two behaviors. In the case of all children, other behaviors needing modification can be added as time goes on and you have experienced success with the system.

Sample List for a Four-Year-Old (Limit: Five)
1. Interrupts me on phone
2. Whines
3. Won't pick up toys
4. Fights with sister
5. Won't go to bed on time

Sample List for a Fifteen-Year-Old (Limit: 10)
1. Won't clean room
2. Uses disrespectful body language
3. Procrastinates on homework
4. Always has an excuse
5. Talks on phone too much

Step 2:

Setting Up Your Rules

One reason it is important to have written rules at home is that our adult society depends on written rules. Without them, we would be arguing constantly with one another over what the rules are.

A few years ago my wife was in a car accident in Baton Rouge, Louisiana. Fortunately she was not hurt badly, but she did have to take an ambulance to the hospital. I was in the emergency room with her when a state trooper came in. He called me out of the room and said, "Look, I don't want to upset your wife, but I have to leave a ticket for her because the accident was her fault."

I got a little upset about it, but he said, "Oh, don't worry about it; all you have to do is take this ticket down to the courthouse and pay it. That's all you have to do."

Later, I took the ticket down to the courthouse and stood in line for about twenty minutes; finally I got up to the counter, and the woman behind the counter said, "Can I help you, sir?"

"You certainly may," I replied politely. I passed the ticket across the counter to her, saying, "I need to pay this ticket for my wife."

She glanced at the ticket, passed it back across the counter to me, and even more politely said, "No, I'm sorry, sir, but your wife will have to go to court on this ticket."

I passed that ticket back across the counter to her and said, "No, no, you don't understand. You see, the state trooper told me personally that all I need to do is come down here and pay the ticket."

Again she passed the ticket back across the counter to me and said, "Well, *I'm* telling you *personally* that your wife is going to have to go to court on this ticket."

So I did what you might do: I *shoved* the ticket back across the counter to her, retorting, "Now, you show me where it says that!"

She replied, "I'd be happy to, sir. Let's turn that ticket over. Right on the back it says, 'If it's an accident, you must go to court.' "

The point is, we certainly don't want to get into an argument with our kids over what the rules are, do we? We all know who wins those arguments—at least, all too often. So it's necessary to have at least a few written rules in order to make your family run smoothly.

At the end of this chapter is a list of sample rules you can use to pattern your written rules for your children, turning your list of misbehaviors into some short, easy-to-understand written rules.

The list includes thirty-six sample rules. I'd like to review a few here to give you an idea of the types of rules I'm talking about. I'll also explain why we have these particular rules in our family.

The number one rule on this list was the number one rule in my family when I grew up, and I'll bet it was the number one rule in lots of other families as well. In our family, this was not a written rule, but it didn't really need to be because it was very clearly and effectively communicated to us on a daily basis. This rule states: "Disrespectful language is not allowed."

In the 1950s and 1960s, children were not allowed to be disrespectful to their parents. Under no circumstances could they go to school and be disrespectful to a teacher. Heaven help you if you went to church and were disrespectful to someone there. Respect was an incredibly important issue to our parents' generation.

Even though it's still a very important issue to our generation of parents, it's not being communicated very effectively to our children. Kids today sometimes say such disrespectful things that it leaves parents almost aghast. Parents respond with things like "What in the world gives you the idea you can talk to me like that?"

Let's think for a moment. What *is* giving our kids the idea that they can talk to us like that? Could it be perhaps that they're spending time at their friends' houses, where they hear their friends getting away with being disrespectful to their parents? That's one possibility. Could it also be that our children are turning on the television and watching all kinds of sitcoms and cartoons in which disrespectful comments are key to the comedy? That's a real possibility as well, isn't it?

Disrespect between parents and children is being used as comedy in the media. Disrespect between teachers and students is being used as comedy. In fact, disrespect between brothers and sisters, even friends, is being used as comedy. Our kids are being bombarded with the message that not only is it perfectly okay to be disrespectful to the people in their lives, it's *fun*. Unfortunately, they are even getting the message that you can become popular—in fact, an admired leader—by being disrespectful.

Our kids are picking up this message at very early ages. Here is a case in point. I was on an airplane, sitting next to a young woman. She asked me what I did for a living. I told her about my work with families and she said, "Well, then, can I ask you about something my three-year-old daughter is doing?"

I said, "Sure, what's she doing?"

The young mother replied seriously, "Lately, every time I ask her to do something, she tells me to shut up."

"For heaven's sake, where's she getting that from?" I queried.

"It's interesting that you ask," replied the mother, "because I just discovered the answer a couple of days ago. I was walking through the living room while my daughter was watching her favorite movie, *Toy Story*. And there was Buzz telling Woody, 'Shut up, shut up!' I was horrified!"

I told this story in South Dakota at a Smart Discipline workshop. During the break, a young father came up to me and said, "I nearly fell out of my chair when you told that story. Just last night I told my four-year-old son, Eric, 'It's time to get ready for bed; let's go upstairs.' Without blinking, he looked up at me and said, 'No, Daddy!'

" 'What do you mean, no?' I demanded. To which he innocently quipped, 'No, Daddy, because you're an idiot!' Where did he get it? Same place—*Toy Story*."

During that same seminar another father came up to me at the end of the break and said, "I just thought you'd like to know I went to check on the kids being babysat back in the church day care center. And they're all having a real good time watching . . . *Toy Story!*"

Unfortunately, every time a child is allowed to be disrespectful to the people in his life, he loses a little bit of respect for those people. Not a lot. Just a little bit, but those little bits add up over a period of time. A child who is continually allowed to be disrespectful ends up losing all respect for those people. Once that happens, that child is a thousand miles down the road toward being totally and completely out of control. Such children are very difficult to reach at that point.

My wife and I include in this issue of disrespect the use of disrespectful body language. Those of you with kids between the ages of ten and sixteen know exactly what I'm talking about. It can drive parents crazy.

Years ago, when I was traveling around America holding my big Up With Youth weekend rallies with four or five hundred kids, I looked forward to finding all kinds of interesting differences between the kids being raised in the Deep South, the kids being raised in the Midwest, and the kids being raised on the East or West Coast. Also, I thought I would find all kinds of interesting differences between the kids raised in the rural areas of our country and the kids raised in our cities.

I was wrong about all that. I discovered that our kids are very much the same no matter where they're being raised. One of the ways in which they are much the same is in their disrespectful body language.

I tried to figure out how a child being raised in Baton Rouge, Louisiana, could act exactly the same as a child being raised, say, in Chicago, Illinois. I finally figured it out after a couple of years of studying and observing children.

When children get to middle school age, they start attending their own seminars. You have seen them in these seminars. All you have to do is go to a Friday night football game or basketball game where you see the little groups of middle-school students standing around talking to one another. Are they watching the game? No, they couldn't care less about the game; they're in a seminar.

These seminars also explain why your kids are so desperate to go to the mall. "What do you mean, you need to go to the mall?" you say. "You've spent all your money, and I'm certainly not giving you any more!" Well, these seminars, you see, are free.

What do they learn in these seminars? They learn the three basic rules of communication with their parents. Rule number one declares: When your parents are talking to you, do not let them look you in the eye. Whatever it takes, avoid eye contact at all costs.

Rule number two: Roll your own eyes as frequently as possible.

I've often wondered whether they actually learn exercises to strengthen the eye-rolling muscles!

Rule number three: End every conversation with statements like "Whatever! Do whatever you want; you never do what I want, anyway!"

These seminars are, of course, just fantasy. But I think the point is valid. Disrespect today is rampant, and it is spreading from child to child at alarming rates. If parents are to have any chance of stopping this progression, then all forms of disrespect must be attended to, whether verbal or nonverbal. This can be covered with one simple written rule: No disrespectful language—verbal *or* nonverbal.

Here's another very important rule in our family: Chores must be done by six P.M. To know why this rule is so important in our family, you have to know a little bit about my wife. Nydia is one of these women who always want things to be cleaned up, picked up, and neat at all times. You know the type. Won't go to bed at night until the whole house is cleaned up, picked up, and neat. Won't leave for work in the morning until the whole house is cleaned up, picked up, and neat.

As for me, I'm still trying to figure out how in the world the house gets so messed up in the middle of the night. How does that happen? It's still a mystery to me and likely will always remain so. In any case, before we had Smart Discipline, our days would typically go like this. We'd send the kids to school in the morning and make them promise to come straight home after school to do their chores and get started on their homework. We would get home from work about five-thirty or six o'clock. If it was a school day, we would walk into the kitchen and find things on the kitchen table like schoolbooks, dirty socks, and notes from the teacher that we should have seen about a month ago. Then we would look at the counter and find the bread air-drying there.

I would rescue what was left of the bread. Standing there with the stale bread in my hand, I'd say to myself, What am I supposed to do with this stale bread? Oh, I know. I'll just stick it back in the bag and make the kids eat it. That will teach them a lesson! But the next time they want a piece of bread, do they eat that stuff? No, they stick it right back in the bag, saying, "I'm not eating that stuff, it's stale! Mom and Dad'll eat it. I'll just open the fresh loaf."

After I put the bread away, I'd poke my head in the refrigerator to see if I could find something for supper. That's when I'd see it: "Oh, no, red punch spilled all over the floor, darn it all!" I'd ask my reflection in the refrigerator door who would do such a thing and just leave it there for someone else to clean up, but it (my reflection) would just stare blankly back at me, much as my kids would do when I asked them such questions.

Once I got that cleaned up, it would be time to go around the kitchen and close the drawers, cupboard doors, and microwave oven door. Walking farther into the house, I would find all three TVs on. But was anyone watching television? Of course not. The kids would be at their friends' houses, watching a few of those thirty-six thousand hours of television. And most certainly the chores wouldn't be done. I'm sure you can now see why we desperately needed a rule that says "Your chores must be done by six P.M."

The next rule on our list was one we created purely in self-defense. Homework must be done by nine P.M. Before we had this rule and the Smart Discipline System, we endured hassles over homework every night. Fifteen minutes' worth of homework would take five hours to do. Not five pleasant hours, mind you; five hours of pulling teeth.

Things like this would happen way too often: After supper, our kids, being the all-American kids they are, would ask that question that you hear in your home so often: May we turn on the TV now? Being all-American parents, how do you think we responded? That's right—we asked, "Is your homework done?"

In response, our all-American kids would respond, "Sure." Or, "I didn't have any today, Dad." Or, "I did it at school." Or, "I did it on the bus." Doesn't it bother you just a little when your children say things like this? I mean, wouldn't it be nice if just once they said something like "You're absolutely right. I've got way too much homework tonight. Look, could we just leave the TV off tonight?" I don't know about you, but we are still waiting to hear that one.

Instead, we would accept their response and tell them it was okay to turn on the television. Finally, at nine or ten o'clock, we'd get the kids off to bed and we'd sit down to watch a little television ourselves. Invariably, at about ten o'clock one of the kids would come out of the bedroom and say something like "Dad, would you help me with my homework, please?"

I'd respond, "Darn it, you told me your homework was done! What's the problem?"

"I'm sorry, Dad, but I forgot something."

"Well, what—what did you forget?"

"Don't get mad, Dad, but I've got this major project due."

And when do you suppose it was due? Tomorrow, of course! So, at ten o'clock at night I would be sent out to find that great big piece of white cardboard with a reminder not to forget the glue and the glitter.

We don't do this anymore. When you think about it, any homework done after nine o'clock at night is unlikely to be done properly anyway. For the younger kids I suggest an earlier deadline for homework to be done (more on this in chapter 12: "Three Effective Homework Guidelines").

Getting our kids to follow this next rule has made all the effort my wife and I ever put into Smart Discipline worthwhile: No fighting or bickering. About 87 percent of the insanity in our family was attributable to fighting and bickering. Things like this would happen: One of the kids would be sitting in the living room reading a book, minding her own business. Another of our children would come through the living room and cuff her on the head.

Shocked, I'd demand, "Now, why did you do that?"

"It wasn't my fault, Dad. She knows how much it aggravates me for her to be sitting there so peaceful-like. I just couldn't stand it, Dad. She was aggravating me on purpose!"

Sometimes I would come home from work and we'd decide to take the kids down to the Piccadilly Cafeteria for supper. Before we'd even pulled out of the driveway, we'd hear things like "Dad, he's looking at me!" Or "Dad, he's touching me!" And "Well, she's breathing my air!"

During the drive across town, the fighting and bickering would escalate to intolerable levels. In frustration, either my wife or I would blurt out the age-old warning: "Don't make me stop this van! If I have to stop, you're going to be in big, big trouble!" How nice it was when we put Smart Discipline in place with the "No fighting or bickering" rule.

The last rule I'm going to mention here is one my wife came up with. Nydia realized we couldn't have a rule for every little thing, so this one covers a lot of ground. It says you must do what you are asked, the first time you're asked. Wouldn't it be wonderful if you could just ask your children to do something and they complied the first time? Even better, to get them to do so willingly? This is exactly what the Smart Discipline System is designed to do.

Now it's your turn to make your own list of written rules. To get started, I suggest you review the sample rules that follow. Then use your lists of misbehaviors to help guide you to make your own list.

Remember, in the Smart Discipline System, you can have up to five rules for a child between the ages of three and eight. Up to ten rules can be used for children ages nine and over. However, if your child is either ADD or ADHD, regardless of his age, start out with no more than one or two rules. In all cases, you can change or add other rules once you experience success with the system.

Please note: If there are wide differences in ages among your children, you will likely have different lists of rules for different children.

Sample Rules for Three- to Eight-Year-Olds (Limit: 5)
1. Toys must be put away by seven o'clock every night.
2. You must stay in the yard.
3. No hitting.
4. No screaming.
5. You must be in bed by eight P.M.
6. No roughhousing.
7. No fighting and bickering with_____ .
8. Chores must be done before you go out to play.
9. You may get up only once after you go to bed.
10. You must make your bed before you go to school.
11. No disrespectful language.
12. No lying.
13. You may eat only in the kitchen.
14. Homework must be done and checked before the television can be turned on.
15. No television in the morning before school.

Sample Rules for Nine- to Sixteen-Year-Olds (Limit: 10)
1. No disrespectful language.
2. Chores must be done by six P.M.
3. Homework must be done by nine P.M.
4. No fighting or bickering.

5. No leaving dirty dishes around the house (especially in your room).
6. You must do what you are asked, the first time you're asked.
7. No criticizing the food.
8. You must have permission before you leave the house to go somewhere.
9. Your room must be picked up before you go anywhere.
10. No lying.
11. No swearing or vulgar language.
12. You must be at school on time.
13. No smoking.
14. If you have permission to go somewhere, you must call to get permission to leave that place and go somewhere else.
15. You must ask permission before you take or use something that belongs to another family member.
16. You must be on time for meals.
17. No phone usage after nine P.M. (outgoing or incoming).
18. You must be in by your curfew, which is ten P.M. on weekdays (or school nights during the school year) and midnight on weekends.
19. No television or telephone privileges until your homework is done.
20. No computer privileges until your homework is done (unless you have approval to use it for a homework assignment).
21. No computer usage after ten P.M.

4

Step 3:

Selecting Appropriate Consequences

Once you have selected and written down your rules, you're ready for the next step: Make a list of five privileges that you know to be important to your children. Before we discuss what kinds of privileges might be on that list, let's talk a bit more about how our adult society works, as this will explain the "why" behind this step.

As I've already said, in order for all of us to get along together, we have to have our rules written down. I suppose that when our forefathers were structuring our society, they reasoned something like "We're going to write down the rules, call them laws, tell people what they are, and we'll all get along just fine."

However, pretty quickly, they must have realized that in order to motivate people to follow the rules, they had to have a system in which people were told that they had to follow the rules, otherwise they would lose their privileges. That's a pretty good system: simple, yet powerful enough to keep almost all of us cooperating with one another.

It's a good thing that we don't run our society the way we run our families. If we did, things like this could happen: Let's say that one Friday evening I'm driving home from work. I have a little time to think and I'm thinking to myself, I wish I had some more money. What would I do if I had some more money? Oh, I know. I'd buy my friend Bob's bass boat! That thing has one of those two-hundred-horse Johnsons on it, and it's faster than fast! I'd have some great weekends if I owned that boat. Then I'd think, Why am I even dreaming about owning that boat? I don't have enough money for that. All my credit cards are charged to the limit. I promised my wife I'd save every extra dollar I could get my hands on so I could take her to Hawaii next summer for our anniversary. I've got seventy-eight, no, I've got eighty-one dollars saved for that. That's not nearly enough.

I say to myself, If I had an extra twenty grand, I could pay off all of my credit cards, buy Bob's bass boat, and still have plenty of money to take my wife to Hawaii.

Then, as I'm driving through town, I spot one of those banks that stay open late on Friday evenings.

Oh, what the heck, says my self-talk. I've got my hunting rifle in the trunk. Just this once. I'll get some money out of the bank the easy way. I pull into the bank's parking lot, get out the rifle, run into the bank, and ever-so-politely say, "Stick 'em up. Give me twenty thousand dollars."

The teller is nice about it. She counts out twenty grand and hands it to me in a bank bag.

Now suppose I'm leaving the bank with that bag of money and my rifle. If our society runs the way we run our families, here's what would happen next. A policeman on the street sees me carrying the rifle and the bag full of money, puts two and two together, and yells, "All right, buster! You turn right around and give that money back. You know better than to take other people's money. Now, you get over there and apologize to that teller. In fact, I'm not letting you out of this bank until you sincerely apologize. Once you're done apologizing, I want you to go straight home and think about what you've done. And don't even think about coming out of your house until you're good and sorry!"

If we ran our society the way we run our families, we would not have much money left in our banks, would we? Actually, I think that as parents we have the authority to allow our children some latitude regarding their misbehavior every once in a while, but if we do it too often, we run a very real risk of teaching our kids that they can act with impunity because there are no consequences for their misbehavior. That's why, to make sure your children know that there are rules in your family as well as consequences for breaking the rules, start by making a list of five privileges that you know to be important to your children.

For younger children, of course, you will have different privileges on the list from those for older ones. For younger children, the list may include privileges like staying up until normal bedtime, playing with favorite toys (some parents include several favorite toys on this list), watching television, playing video games, being on the Internet, snack time, being able to go outside and play, being able to have a friend over to play, or being able to ride their bikes.

With teenagers, it's normally social privileges that are most important—anything that puts them together with their friends. For example, being on the phone with their friends, being on the Internet with their friends, weekend privileges, spending the night at friends' houses, going to the mall, going to the movies, riding their bikes, driving the car, studying with friends, and attending extracurricular activities at school.

If you have any trouble coming up with this list of five privileges, here's a suggestion from a couple in Birmingham, Alabama. After one of my seminars, a mother called and said, "My husband and I were very excited about Smart Discipline after the seminar, so we went home right away and started our lists." But, she said, "we got stuck when we got to this list of five privileges. We didn't have the foggiest idea what to put on it." She continued, "Not to worry, though, because we came up with a solution that worked so well for us, we thought you might want to pass it along."

"Sure," I replied. "What is it?"

She answered, "Well, when we got stuck, we told our children about Smart Discipline and asked what privileges they thought we should consider using. They had all kinds of suggestions!"

I call this "family participation"! Many other parents have validated this approach as surprisingly useful.

By whatever means, then, come up with a list of five privileges for each of your children. Once you have your list, rank them from one to five, with the least important privilege being number one and the most important being number five. As you will see next, these privileges will be used as consequences for breaking rules.

SELECTING CONSEQUENCES FOR
THREE- TO EIGHT-YEAR-OLDS

Make a list of the privileges each child enjoys on a daily basis and has come to take for granted. Then choose five that make the most difference to that particular child. Here is a sample list to choose from:

_____   1. Going outside to play

_____   2. Watching TV

_____   3. Having a friend over

_____   4. Riding bike

_____   5. Favorite toy (you can use different toys for more than one privilege)

_____   6. Going to a friend's house to play

_____   7. Bedtime snack

_____   8. Going to the movies

_____   9. Story time

_____ 10. Video games

_____ 11. Computer time

_____ 12. Other _____

_____ 13. Other _____

_____ 14. Other _____

_____ 15. Other _____

SELECTING CONSEQUENCES FOR
NINE- TO SIXTEEN-YEAR-OLDS

_____   1. Riding bike (or driving car, if older)

_____   2. Having friends over

_____   3. Studying with a friend

_____   4. Extracurricular activities at school

_____   5. Weekend privileges

_____   6. Sleep-over privileges

_____   7. Baby-sitting privileges

_____   8. Going to the movies

_____   9. Going to the mall

_____ 10. Going out at night
_____ 11. Computer privileges
_____ 12. Phone privileges
_____ 13. Video games
_____ 14. Television
_____ 15. Other _____

Once you have selected five privileges for each child, rank them from one to five, with the least important privilege number one and the most important number five. When you've completed your list(s), you will be ready to go on to the next step of setting up your Smart Discipline chart.

Step 4:

Setting Up Your Smart Discipline Chart

At this point you should have selected your rules along with five privileges that are important to each of your children. Now you're ready to set up a Smart Discipline chart for each child. For children ages three to eight, I suggest using a daily chart that you fill out daily. For older children, it is best to use the weekly chart that you fill out each week. For ADD/ADHD children, I suggest using a daily chart regardless of their age. As success with the system progresses, you can move to weekly charts for ADD/ADHD children over the age of nine.

Take a moment now and look at the sample charts. Notice that the daily chart contains eight squares and the weekly chart twelve. Each chart works exactly the same way. In the last five boxes of each chart you'll put those five privileges you listed in the last chapter.

SAMPLE DAILY CHART FOR THREE- TO EIGHT-YEAR-OLDS

Name: _____

Day of Week: _____

A	B	C	Bike D
Friends E	Outside F	TV G	Snack H

Rule of the day:* <u>Pick up your toys</u> _____

Good job yesterday on: <u>Going to bed on time</u> _____

All rules apply, but please pay special attention to this rule today.

DAILY CHART FOR THREE- TO EIGHT-YEAR-OLDS

Name: _____

Day of Week: _____

A	B	C	D͞
E͞	F͞	G͞	H͞

Rule of the day:* _____

_____

Good job yesterday on: _____

_____

_____

All rules apply, but please pay special attention to this rule today.

SAMPLE WEEKLY CHART FOR
NINE- TO SIXTEEN-YEAR-OLDS

Name: _____

From: _____ To: _____
       Date (Sunday)   Date (Saturday)

A	B	C	D	E	F
G	<u>Video</u> Games H	<u>Phone</u> <u>Privileges</u> I	<u>Having</u> <u>Friends</u> <u>Over</u> J	<u>TV</u> K	<u>Weekend</u> <u>Privileges</u> L

Rule of the week:* <u>No disrespectful language</u>

Good job last week on: <u>Being courteous and doing your</u>
<u>chores on time!</u>

All rules apply, but this week please pay special attention to this rule.

WEEKLY CHART FOR
NINE- TO SIXTEEN-YEAR-OLDS

Name: _____

From: _____ To: _____
      Date (Sunday)   Date (Saturday)

A	B	C	D	E	F
G	H	I	J	K	L

Rule of the week:* _____

_____

Good job last week on: _____

_____

_____

All rules apply, but this week please pay special attention to this rule.

On the sample daily chart for the younger children, the least important privilege is in the box marked "D" and the most important privilege is in the box marked "H." Below the chart are the lines for "rule of the day" and "good job yesterday."

The rule of the day is the rule that you especially want your children to pay attention to that day. All of the other rules apply as well, but this is the one that you want to place special emphasis on.

The "good job yesterday" line is to remind you to give your children credit for following the rules you've set in place. Even if your children aren't following the rules perfectly, you should give them credit for doing their best in at least some area of behavior (more on this issue in chapter 7, "Guidelines for Using Smart Discipline").

In the weekly chart for older children, the least important privilege is in the box marked "H" and the most important is in the box marked "L." Also, fill in the blank for the "rule of the week." If you can think of some good behavior from the previous week, fill in the blank for "good job last week." If not, leave it blank during the first week of using the system.

Now that you have perused the samples, photocopy the blank charts that are appropriate to the ages of your children. Then fill them in.

6

Step 5:

Explaining How Smart Discipline Works

Once you've got your charts made up, call a short family meeting to explain Smart Discipline. Bring to this meeting a copy of the rules for each child, along with a sample chart.

Tell your children that you have found something you'd like to try for the family. You may get a few groans of discontent at this point, but ignore them and calmly explain the rules.

Depending on the ages of your children, you will likely get different responses. Young children tend to like structured systems of discipline because of the attention it brings to them. Many will also recognize the system as being something like what their teachers are doing.

Children ten and older will more likely respond negatively to the rules you have read. You will likely hear things like "Hey, these [rules] aren't fair! Who made up these rules, anyway?"

At this point, parents normally want to know if it's okay to let the kids have some input or if it's better to emphasize to their children that parents are responsible for determining the rules.

It is perfectly reasonable to allow children some say in what the rules are. Often, by allowing your children to participate in the creation of the system, they will be more willing participants in its execution. On the other hand, for the parents thinking, Hey, wait a minute! Aren't we the parents? It only makes sense that we should make the rules, the answer is affirmative as well. You can still be a loving parent and say to your kids, "I'm sorry, but in our family parents make the rules."

Whether you choose to allow child participation is up to you. In either case, you will want to establish at this point both that there are going to be rules and exactly what those rules are.

FAMILY MEETING INSTRUCTIONS FOR PARENTS
OF CHILDREN AGES THREE TO EIGHT

After you have reviewed the rules, show your children one of the sample daily Smart Discipline charts you've made up and say something like the following:

- "This is a Smart Discipline chart, and this is how it works."
- "We are going to keep the charts on the refrigerator along with a list of the rules."
- "If you break a rule, I'll tell you what rule you broke and I'll put an X in the box marked 'A.' "
- "If you break another rule, or if you break the same rule again, I'll put an X in the box marked 'B.' "
- "On the daily chart there are three free squares. This means that for the first three rule violations, you won't lose any privileges."
- "The purpose of the Xs in these squares is to warn you that you are headed for negative consequences and had better start following the rules."
- "If you get Xs in the three free squares and then break another rule, an X will be placed in the box marked 'D' and you will lose the privilege listed in that box for the rest of the day."
- "We'll start a new chart every day."

FAMILY MEETING INSTRUCTIONS FOR PARENTS
OF CHILDREN AGES NINE TO SIXTEEN

After you have reviewed the rules, show your children one of the sample weekly Smart Discipline charts you've made up and say something like the following:

- "This is a Smart Discipline chart, and this is how it works."
- "We are going to keep the charts on the refrigerator along with a list of the rules."
- "If you break a rule, I'll tell you what rule you broke and I'll put an X in the box marked 'A.' "

- "If you break another rule, or if you break the same rule again, I'll put an X in the box marked 'B.' "
- "On the weekly chart there are seven free squares. So for the first seven rule violations, you won't lose any privileges."
- "The purpose of the Xs in these squares is to warn you that you are headed for negative consequences and had better start following the rules."
- "If you get Xs in the seven free squares and then break another rule, an X will be placed in the box marked 'H' and you will lose the privilege listed in that box for the rest of the week."
- "We'll start a new chart every week."

Here is some more good news about Smart Discipline: It takes very little explanation. Once you've reviewed the rules and the chart with your children, they will know exactly what you're talking about.

You can expect your kids to try to talk you out of using Smart Discipline. I sometimes think kids think that their purpose in life is to show their parents the errors of their ways and that what they are doing is stupid. They assert that "none of my friends' parents are doing it!"

One of our kids had a very creative way of trying to talk us out of using Smart Discipline. She has one of those great big beautiful smiles. She gave us that million-watt smile and said, "Mom, Dad, look at this smile!"

"Why?" we asked.

To which she replied, "Look at this smile, because it's the last time you're going to see it!"

We chuckled and ignored it, which is what I suggest you do if your children try to talk you out of using Smart Discipline.

Also, as we did with our children, you may want to inform them that if the charts are missing or defaced in any way, you will simply take away *all* of their privileges for the rest of the week (or day, for children on the daily chart). Knowing this, our children never messed with the charts in any way.

Let me tell you how Smart Discipline worked out in our family. The first couple of days the kids broke rules and we put the Xs on the charts. Each time, we told them what rule(s) they broke and informed them that their chart had just been blemished with an X. They pretty much ignored us. Maybe they hoped that we would get discouraged and give up on Smart Discipline.

On Wednesday of the first week, one of our children said, "Dad, I was wondering if I could go to Chris's party on Friday night."

Being the responsible father, I questioned, "What kind of party is it going to be?"

The reply: "It's no big deal, really. We're just, ah, gonna go over to his place after school for pizza, then we're all going to go out bowling together. Would that be all right?"

I'd been preparing for this eventuality all week. "It sounds like a lot of fun," I replied. "Of course you can go. But you'll have to have your weekend privileges."

"What do you mean?" A bewildered look.

"Well," I said, "remember those charts we put on the refrigerator? One of your privileges is your weekend privileges. You'll have to have that in order to go to the party."

All of a sudden the bewildered look was replaced with one of panic. "But Dad, I've already got five Xs on that chart!"

You could almost see the wheels turn in this child's head: *Maybe I'd better go back to my room and get my homework done before nine. Maybe I'd better stop bickering with my sisters. Maybe I'd better take out the garbage when Mom asks me to!*

It's an amazing thing—almost miraculous, in fact—how quickly our children got motivated to follow the rules. We called it a miracle because for years we'd been trying to convince our kids that they were responsible for their own behavior, but they always had a consistent comeback: "Hey, it wasn't my fault!"

Now, all of a sudden, the kids were taking control of their own behavior. And what square do you suppose they stopped misbehaving on? On the weekly chart, it was "G."

I was amazed at their precision control. For two months, not one single child lost one single privilege. They would always somehow manage to stop misbehaving just before they lost a privilege.

I never really minded it, though, when our kids broke a few of the rules and then stopped themselves from misbehaving before they lost privileges. It's a wonderful moment when you can experience your children stopping themselves from misbehaving. It shows that they are learning self-control and self-discipline, and this is indeed a great event for both parents and children.

Here is a case in point. One young mother told me, "I've been using Smart Discipline with my ten-year-old son and seven-year-old daughter very successfully for the last month. But I got concerned last night when I was cooking supper and heard my son take off after his sister because she wouldn't relinquish the remote control. I was just about to set down the soup ladle and intervene when I heard my son say, 'Ya know, we better stop this before we get another X on that stupid chart!' "

This is a good thing. This is the beginning of learning self-control!

7

Guidelines for
Using Smart Discipline

You will probably find that your children will respond to the Smart Discipline system in one of several ways. Some children hate to get a single X on their charts. These children are normally well behaved and will go out of their way to comply with the rules.

Other children will break a few rules but will usually be careful to stop breaking them before they lose any privileges. Still others, typically the defiant ones, will break enough rules to lose all their privileges almost immediately. These children are testing their parents to see what they will do.

The answer: Take away all privileges until the chart starts over again. If they continue to break rules after they've lost all their privileges, put them in time-out in their rooms. Some question this tactic because bedrooms are often stocked with all kinds of fun things. That's okay. I don't view time-out so much as punishment as getting the child out of your hair for a little while. Sending them to their rooms also makes the statement that you can't expect to misbehave and stay with the rest of the family.

Here are a few other guidelines to follow to make the use of Smart Discipline easier and more effective.

- **Refrain from giving warnings or second chances.** For example, do not say, "You had better stop fighting with your brother or I'm going to put an X on your chart." Instead, identify what rule was broken and put the X on the chart. Certainly children deserve some warning that they are headed for trouble, but this is built into the system with "free" squares. Also, by putting the X on their charts without warning, you are teaching your children that you mean business the first time—without screaming and yelling!

- **If you don't know which child broke a rule, give all of them Xs.** Too often, parents take on the role of detective, looking for proof of who did what. This is not productive. While it is desirable in a family to be as fair as possible when determining blame, it is a misconception that you need proof in order to take action. You do not. Proof is for courts. Good judgment is for families. So use your best judgment to determine who did what. If you're still uncertain, give everyone an X. It may not seem fair to your children, but it will teach them that you are not about to let misbehavior continue just because someone is smart enough not to get caught red-handed.

- **Give your children appreciation for the rules they adhere to.** Adults hate it when someone points out only what they are doing wrong. In fact, they get indignant and demoralized when it happens. Children are the same way. Sometimes both children and adults can end up thinking, Why bother following the rules at all? So make sure that each time you start a new chart, you fill in the "good job" blank and mention it to your child.

- **Leave off the lecture.** When your children break a rule, inform them of what rule they broke and put an X on their charts. Lecturing is likely to worsen the situation rather than improve it. One reason you're using this system is that you're probably tired of lecturing and know that it doesn't work. Besides, if you leave off the lecture, your children will tend to do a better job of lecturing themselves about breaking rules. This is much more desirable and effective than a lecture from a parent.

- **Note in the box what rule was broken.** When you put an X on a chart, you may also want to note what rule was broken. This can serve as a reminder to you and to your children of why the X was given.

- **Fill in the rule of the day or rule of the week space.** All rules apply, but tell your children that this is the rule that you especially want them to concentrate on. For example: "This week I want you to pay special attention to refraining from fighting and bickering."

The last guideline I am going to mention is this: When a privilege is lost, *do not give it back until the chart starts over again.* This is a very, very important guideline, but a very, very difficult one for our generation of parents to follow. It's both important and difficult because parents are in the bad habit of handling things as in the following scenario.

Suppose I'm coming home from work one night and I walk into the house just in time to hear one of my daughters talking back to her mom again. This has been happening all too often, and I've had it, so I call her into the kitchen and nag at her: "How many times have I had to talk to you about talking back to your mom? Maybe a thousand, two thousand times? It's been a lot, hasn't it? Well, one of the things we know for sure is that the talking hasn't helped, has it?"

"No," she replies as she hangs her head low.

"No, it hasn't," I reaffirm. "So, I guess I'm going to have to do something dramatically different. To be honest with you, I don't know what to do with you anymore, because nothing seems to work. But I've got to do something, so I guess I'll just have to ground you. How about we say, oh, I don't know, how about a month? What do you think? . . . No? . . . Oh, I see, you think this is funny. Well then, you are really going to have a good laugh. Two months! That's right, two months! You can tell your friends not to be calling here or coming here. And do not give me any garbage about how you *need* to be studying with your friends, because you're studying alone, young lady! In fact, by the time we're done with this, your friends will be calling you the Lone Rangeress.

"One more thing. I want you to go find your mother and get all of the crying, all of the whining, and all of the 'not fair' stuff out of the way, because I'm sticking to my guns this time. You can count on it!"

So what happens? Too often the scenario ends like this. It's Saturday morning, about seven o'clock. A racket in the living room awakens me. I go out to investigate, and there's my daughter vacuuming. At ten o'clock in the morning she's helping her mother do all of the chores around the house. At two o'clock in the afternoon I look outside and there she is on a stepladder washing all of the windows. By three o'clock in the afternoon she's got the vacuum out again, vacuuming my car. When she gets done she bounces into the house and asks happily, "Daddy, did I do a good job around the house today?"

What do I respond? "Sure did! Your mother and I are so proud of you."

"Daddy," she says, "when you grounded me the other night, I bet you didn't remember that it's my best friend Debbie's big party tonight, did you?"

I say, "Well, no. I didn't remember that. That's really too bad, isn't it?"

She replies, "Now hang on, Daddy. Just hear me out. Keep an open mind; you're always telling me to keep an open mind! How about this, Daddy? Every Saturday for the next three months I'm going to get up and do all of the chores around the house. Whatever Mom needs done, I'm gonna do it. She can even leave me a list on Friday night so I can make sure I get up early to get everything done. And how about this? You can ground me for three months, not two, but three months, Daddy, 'cause I've been bad. I don't want to ever sass my mother again, Daddy! How about that? All that punishment, Daddy, but please, please let me go to that party tonight!"

This child knows that if she can get me to say yes, all bets are off. She won't have to do another lick of work around the house. She won't be grounded for another minute. She knows it and we know it! But despite knowing it, what do I do? The same thing most parents do: give in and say, "Well, all right, you can go to that party tonight. But I hope you learned your lesson, young lady!"

Yes, she learned a lesson. The trouble is, it's not a good one. She learned that she can act with impunity because she can always get out of the consequences for any misbehavior.

When parents let their children out of consequences, they typically do so for one of two reasons. First, they do it because they love their children dearly and want to believe that their child has indeed learned an appropriate lesson and will not repeat the behavior. Second, parents give in because of the ruckus the child is creating in response to the punishment.

But letting children out of negative consequences can create further problems. Kids learn pretty quickly how to escape punishment. Each time they do, the skids are greased for them to repeat the same and other misbehaviors. So I recommend that parents think long and hard before they do the supposedly "kind" thing and remove consequences. While I realize it's tough to watch your children feel anguish over their mistakes and punishment, it is a far tougher thing to end up with a child out of control because you did not do so.

8

Common Questions and Answers About
Implementing the Smart Discipline System

Tens of thousands of parents use the Smart Discipline System. Through its use, a number of common questions have popped up. Those questions and my responses are presented here. It is my hope that you will be able to find any answers you might need in this section. If not, e-mail your question to larry@smartdiscipline.com.

Q. What about sports? If a child is committed to playing in an upcoming game, aren't you punishing the whole team if you don't let him play because he misbehaved?

A. No, you are not penalizing the team. Your son penalized the team by misbehaving when he knew that his participation in sports was contingent on his following the rules. For some children, sports are incredibly important. Those children will be highly motivated to follow the rules if they know their parents are serious about disallowing participation in sports when the rules are not adhered to. I would also like to point out that professional athletes are given rules that must be followed. They are told that the consequence for certain rule violations (like coming in drunk after curfew) will be punished by exclusion from the next game.

Q. What about the use of time-out? Does it play a part in Smart Discipline?

A. Yes. A child can be put into time-out for any rule violation at any time. Even if the X is being put in a free or warning square, you can impose a time-out. To me, sending a child to her room for time-out isn't so much punishment as it is a way to cool down the situation. Doing so allows both of you to have some time to calm down. It also gives your child the message that if she is going to misbehave, she can't be with the rest of the family.

Q. What if parents can identify only two or three privileges? We live in the country, and our children don't have many privileges.

A. There are several remedies for this. The first is to modify the chart, having the same number of free squares but fewer boxes for privileges. Or, if your children have a number of favorite toys, you may be able to use several of them as different privileges. Finally, you may want to delay starting the use of the system for a week. During that time, pay attention to how your children spend their free time. This may give you a number of additional ideas.

Q. What about all of the paper that gets wasted by having always to make up new charts? Is there a better way?

A. I have a couple of thoughts on this. First, my wife and I liked to keep the charts in a file so we could review progress together and identify patterns of misbehavior that needed addressing. So we preferred having hard copies we could keep. Others prefer using magnetic erasable charts. These can be purchased by calling our office at 1-800-255-3008 or by visiting our Web site, smartdiscipline. com.

Q. What about rewards? Is it okay to reward our children for their good behavior?

A. Sure, as long as the rewards are not set up as bribes. In other words, it is perfectly okay to spontaneously tell your children that you are going to treat them to something special because they have been so good lately. This is a loving and wonderful thing to do as a parent. What is not okay is to tell your children that if they behave, you will give them a reward. That is called bribery, and it may work in the short run, but in the long run it will backfire. Kids quickly figure out that either they can bargain for a bigger and better reward or they can choose to misbehave and adopt an "I don't care" attitude about not getting the promised reward. You can avoid these traps by using spontaneous rewards on an occasional basis.

Q. Is it okay to erase an X from a child's chart for good behavior?

A. No. Children need to learn that they must face the consequences of their misbehavior. To give them an "out" is to teach them that they can act with impunity because they can always get out of the consequences. Many parents believe that they are being kind and loving by letting their children escape consequences. This is not so. As difficult as it is to see your children suffer, it is much more difficult later if the child gets out of control because he thinks he can wriggle out of consequences by being good.

Q. Should I make my children put their own Xs on their charts if they break a rule?

A. No. The charts should be marked only by the parents and should be off-limits to the children. It's a matter of image. Keeping the charts under parental control tells your children that this is serious business. Also, when you think about it, would a state trooper hand you his tablet of tickets and tell you to fill one out?

Q. Should parents have a chart? Wouldn't that be the fair thing to do?

A. I don't think so. I think the message to children needs to be, "We are the parents, you are the children. The parents are in control, not the children." However, if your point is that parents need to be good role models and set good examples for their behavior, then I agree most heartily. But this can and should be done without a chart.

Q. I have a two-year-old and a five-year-old. The youngest is too young to have a chart, but my oldest complains that this is unfair.

A. Every child I have ever known learns at the earliest of ages to play the "unfair" card when something is not to her liking. When this happens, I suggest a standard response of "It's because of the difference in ages." Nothing more, nothing less. If you make this your one and only response to the "unfair" mantra, you will save yourself a lot of parental grief. And your children will learn very quickly that whining that something is unfair won't get them what they want.

Q. I have an eight-year-old and a ten-year-old. The youngest should be on a daily chart and the older on a weekly chart. Would it be okay to have both on a weekly chart for continuity's sake?

A. Yes, as long as your younger child is not ADD or ADHD. If she is, then I would keep them both on the daily chart.

Q. My four-year-old is hyperactive. He loses all of his privileges by mid-morning. Is it okay to have a morning and an afternoon chart?
A. Yes. This is a creative solution. And I might add that the Smart Discipline System is meant to be flexible so parents can modify it to fit the needs of their children.

Q. My seven-year-old is often pretty good during the day but tends to misbehave more when he is tried at night, so he doesn't lose his privileges until bedtime. Is it okay to take away his privileges for the next day?
A. Yes. Just make sure to tell him that it will work that way.

Q. My daughter is smart. She waits until Saturday and then breaks all kinds of rules because she knows the weekly chart will start over again on Sunday and she'll get her privileges back. Is there a way of closing this loophole?
A. If this is a continual problem, sit down with her when everything is calm. Explain to her that you notice this pattern. Tell her that if it continues, any privilege lost on Saturday will not be returned until a week from Sunday. This should take care of the problem.

Q. What should I do if a child loses all of his privileges by Wednesday and continues to break rules?
A. Send him to time-out. Since he is on a weekly chart, I assume he is over the age of eight, so I would tell him that every time he breaks a rule after he's already lost his privileges, he will have to spend half an hour in his room.

Q. My daughter loses all of her privileges the first day and says she doesn't care. It's exasperating. What can I do to counteract this tactic?
A. Many children play the "I don't care" card because their parents are likely to throw up their hands and give in and let the child do whatever she wants. To trump the "I don't care" card, tell your child, "Caring doesn't matter. The only thing that matters is that you follow the rules. If you do not do so, you will lose your privileges, but caring

does not matter!" This response will shock your child. She will probably be aghast that you don't care that she doesn't care. And she will learn that in order to have her privileges, she must behave. Persistence will give you the results you want. Sooner or later your child will want her privileges back and will start behaving in order to get them.

Q. My husband and I have started using your Smart Discipline System. We were wondering what to do when our children become defiant when we take away their privileges for not following the rules. I really want this program to work for our family. The boys are fourteen and sixteen, and things have gotten worse this summer. With their insults and cursing at us, we are constantly taking away their privileges. I have a history of chronic fatigue, and these family stresses are really exhausting me. We would appreciate any advice you can give us.

A. The most frequent response to discipline is defiance. The reason: Children—and especially teenagers—know that if they hassle their parents enough, they will most likely give in and back off the discipline for the sake of peace in the family. Now that you know this, I would suggest that you print out both your question and my response and have a family meeting. Discuss what middle ground can be found. Let your children know that you want and need peace, but not at the price of misbehavior and defiance. Get your teenagers' views on things. Ask for their feedback on the rules and what they think should be the consequences for breaking the rules. If they refuse meaningful participation in the process, tell them that despite your fatigue and their defiance, you will keep the rules and consequences just the way they are now. Then tell them how much you love them!

Q. What if my child gets an X for breaking a rule and then breaks the same rule again?

A. Give him another X. However, you may also want to send him to time-out. Sometimes a child gets locked into a defiant behavior pattern and it is best to get him away from the rest of the family for a while to break the pattern. You can, by the way, send a child to time-out at any time you think appropriate, even if you put an X in a "free" square.

Q. The other day I asked my son to take out the garbage and he said, "No, just put an X on my chart." I said no way and made him do it anyway. He claims this was unfair. Was it?

A. You were right. Children should not be given the choice of whether or not to do what they are supposed to do. However, make sure that you are explicit in your expectations about when something must be done. If you mean right away, say so. If the timing is flexible, you can say something like "Taking the garbage out is not an option. You have to take it out, but if you like, we can talk about when you are going to do it." Then give an X if it is not done at that time. If he still does not do it, tell him you are setting the buzzer for ten minutes and if it is not done by the time the buzzer goes off, you will place another X on his chart. If this still does not work, suspend all privileges and send him to time-out until he decides to comply.

Q. My children live with their mother and are at my house only on the weekends. Can I use the Smart Discipline System effectively in this short amount of time?

A. Modify the charts into two-day charts. You could modify the daily chart, making it last for the weekend. You could also tell your children that if they lose their privileges on Sunday, they will not get them back until the following Sunday. In other words, the following Saturday they would be without their privileges.

Q. My children are at their father's house on the weekends, so loss of weekend privileges is no threat to them. What can I do?

A. Don't worry about it. Just concentrate on privileges that they have during the week at your house.

Q. My former husband and I share custody of our two children. Half the time they are with him and half the time with me. If the children lose privileges while at my house, should I ask their father to take them away at his house?

A. This depends on his attitude. You can ask, and if he is supportive, then go ahead. If not, don't worry about it. Just modify the system to account for the time the children are with you.

Q. My child is too young to read, so I paste pictures from magazines and catalogs on her charts to represent her privileges. It works great for her, and I thought I would pass the idea along.

A. What a great idea! Thanks for sharing.

Q. One of my children is so well behaved that I don't see a need for a chart. Her younger brother, on the other hand, is the terror of the neighborhood and definitely needs a chart. Should I have a chart for her anyway?

A. Yes. She can take pride in not violating the rules and having a "clean" chart.

Q. The first week we started Smart Discipline, our children's behavior got worse, not better. What did we do wrong?

A. Nothing. Another card that some children play on their parents is the "revenge" card. Some children have learned that if they punish their parents with more bad behavior, their parents will let them out of their punishment. To trump this card, sit down with your children and tell them that you notice that their behavior gets worse when they are being punished. Tell them that this is their choice, but for as long as they choose to misbehave, you will have to withhold their privileges.

Q. My child has attention deficit disorder with hyperactivity. Will Smart Discipline work with him, and, if so, are there any things I should do differently?

A. Yes, Smart Discipline works well with children who have ADD and ADHD. Children with this condition respond positively to the structure and predictability that Smart Discipline provides. To start, though, use just one or two rules and the daily chart, regardless of your child's age. Keep everything else about the system the same. As you have success with the system, add a rule at a time. Eventually you can move to the weekly chart. Children with ADD/ADHD typically are very bright and learn how to use their condition to get away with misbehaving. However, given set rules and consequences, it is surprising how well they can learn to control their behavior.

Q. What if one of my children does something really bad but has a clean chart? Should I just put an X in a free square and not punish him for what he did?

A. No. If, in your judgment, one of your children's behaviors is way out of line, then punish him according to your best judgment. When you get hit with the "Hey, that's not fair!" card, respond with, "Some behavior is so intolerable that it demands more of a response than an X on a chart. In my estimation, this was one of those behaviors."

Q. On the weekly chart for older children, there are seven free or warning squares. Isn't that a lot of rules to allow a child to break before you punish her?

A. It might seem so. However, if you think about it, most parents yell, threaten, and lecture much more than seven times before they take action. Besides, if the behavior is really bad, you can punish outside of the system, as I mentioned in the previous question. You can also put a child in time-out for any rule violation, even if the X is going in a free square.

Q. I have three children at home. Two are in college and one is in high school. Should they all have charts? If not, what do I do when my teenager points out that we never did this kind of thing with her older brothers and asks why she should have to do it?

A. The college students should not be on a chart. There is only one consequence for not obeying the rules when you are over the age of eighteen and living at home: moving out. As for your daughter, simply tell her that you wish you could use a chart with them, but they are too old. Also, tell her that you wish you had had these charts when they were younger, but you can't do anything about that now.

Q. My children spend time at their grandparents' house almost daily. The trouble is, my parents don't discipline them. Then, when the kids get home, they are wild. Is there a way that Smart Discipline can help?

A. Here are two possibilities. The first is to explain Smart Discipline to your parents and ask for their cooperation. If they are willing, set up the system at their house so that the children will lose privileges both there and at home. If your parents won't go along, set up the system at your house. Explain to your children in particular that you are going to expect good behavior when they return from their grandparents'. If not, you will put Xs on their charts and remove privileges as need be.

Q. I have a child who goes out of her way to get her brothers into trouble. She is a master at misbehaving and putting all the blame on them. Most of the time I literally can't tell who did what. What's the solution here?

A. You are not running a court of law. Therefore, you don't need proof of who is misbehaving. Instead, use your best judgment. If you think you know who did what, put the Xs on the charts accordingly. If you simply don't know, give everyone an X. In so doing, it's true an innocent child may get punished. However, knowing that this can happen causes children to put pressure on their siblings to behave.

Q. How can I get my spouse to go along with Smart Discipline?

A. The best way to get any reluctant spouse to try something is to go ahead and set it up and start doing it. As the system starts to work, she may well dive in and go along with it.

Q. My children misbehave in the car and away from home more than anywhere else. How do I use Smart Discipline away from home?

A. Take pens and some paper with you. Tell your children what the rules are when in the car and where you are going. Then explain that you will keep track of rule violations and will put Xs on their charts when you get home. If you are going away for an extended amount of time, take the charts with you. Explain any appropriate rule changes and privileges they could lose while you are away. Then implement your system. One note of caution, though. Being away from home makes some children anxious, and they become cranky. If you have a child like this, take it into account and don't be too picky.

Q. I have a fourteen-year-old son who is resentful and defiant. Won't imposing rules and consequences just make the situation worse?

A. Initially, perhaps. But if you stick with it, he will most likely get with the program and start behaving. Privileges are incredibly important to teenagers. They will usually comply with the rules in order to be with their friends and to do "their own thing."

Q. What should I do if a child loses a privilege like television or telephone and I come home and catch her cheating?

A. I suggest taking away privileges only for periods of time when you are home to monitor compliance. Demanding compliance when you are not there will only invite your child to sneak around. However, tell them that if they cheat while you are at home, that will constitute a rule violation for which Xs will be placed on charts and corresponding privileges will be taken away.

Q. My wife and I are finding it hard to deal with disrespect from our two teenage boys. We have set up a list of rules that includes a rule about disrespect. But we find it hard to control because the incidents are increasing in frequency. Help!

A. Let me ask you a question. What would you do if your sons came into the living room and dropped a pile of dirt on the floor? Like most parents, you would admonish them, make them clean it up, and explain what the consequences will be if they do it again. One thing is for sure—you would not under any circumstances allow this behavior to continue. You know it, and your teenagers know it, too. They are very aware that dumping dirt on the floor of the living room will not be tolerated.

So why, might you ask, are your children so willing to follow a rule about not dumping dirt in the house, while they willfully and repeatedly break the rule about no disrespectful language?

The answer is fairly simple. You have taught your children that you will never allow the dumping of dirt in the house, so they don't do it. In the same vein, you have also taught your children that you will tolerate their disrespectful language, albeit not on purpose. Like a number of parents of teens, you now find yourself at the point where the disrespectful language has become intolerable. It's time to teach your children that, like bringing dirt into the house, disrespectful language will not be tolerated.

I suggest starting by meeting with your teens to discuss the problem. Own up to the fact that you have been lax in tolerating disrespectful language. Give some examples of the kind of language that is of concern to you. Then ask for their input and ideas on how disrespectful language can completely be eradicated from your home.

Finally, promise your teens two things. First, that you will not say disrespectful things to them. Second, that you will never again allow them to say or do anything disrespectful to anyone in the family without your reprimanding them.

Then follow through. In between times, be sure to point out and express appreciation for the positive things your teens say and do (as you will see in the next chapter, the effects of doing so, over time, will be dramatic!).

PART TWO

Bringing Out the Best in Your Children

9

Instilling
Positive Beliefs

There are two sides to discipline. One side is made up of rules and consequences. Having these gives children a strong foundation and a sense of direction. It also motivates them to follow the rules even when they would sometimes like to do otherwise.

The other side of discipline involves instilling positive beliefs in children. Children who have positive beliefs about themselves behave better than children who have negative beliefs about themselves. How do I know this is true? From years of working with children and observing them. The ones with high self-esteem and self-confidence consistently were happier, better behaved and more well mannered than children who had low self-esteem and self-confidence.

This is not to say that all children with low self-esteem are badly behaved. On the contrary, some are very well behaved. However, by and large children with behavior problems tend to have low self-esteem.

I have never met a parent who didn't want their children to have high self-esteem. Parents instinctively know that their children will be much better off if they have a positive sense of their self-worth. I also think that many adults suffer the ill effects of low self-esteem and very much want to spare their children from them.

In this chapter I explain the step-by-step process by which children pick up beliefs about themselves, both positive and negative. I'll share a true story of how I picked up a belief about myself when I was a child. Then I will lay out a very powerful process for you to use to instill positive beliefs in your children.

THE BELIEF PROCESS

The first step in what I call the Belief Process starts for children when they are very young and continues throughout their childhood and even into their adult years. In this step, they gather information about themselves.

Children get this from all kinds of sources. A lot of them get it from brothers and sisters, Grandma and Grandpa make observations, and children are sent to school, where their teachers give them still more information about themselves. Primarily, though, children look to their parents for information about themselves while they are growing up.

Parents give children all kinds of information, but most of the time they pay little attention to the information they are dishing out. Things like the following will happen frequently. A parent will be in a grocery store with a daughter and will bump into an acquaintance. It is only natural for the parent to introduce the child and say a few things about her. What is said often goes something like "I would like you to meet my daughter Sally. Sally is my really smart child. She gets all As in school. My wife and I think one day she's going to be the valedictorian of her class. The first thing she does when she comes home from school is her homework. I'm just really proud of Sally; she always has such a positive attitude about everything!" You can imagine Sally soaking up all that positive information about herself.

Another time, though, the conversation goes very differently. Let's say a father is at the store with his son when he meets an acquaintance. The father says, "This is my son Jason. Jason! Go put that back before you break it! Ah, that kid! He's out of control. I don't know how his teachers put up with him. He's just a troublemaker. And homework—what a joke. We've given up on Jason in school. . . . How old? Well, he's seven, but he acts more like a two-year-old. I've got to admit, though, he is cute, don't you think? Come here, Jason, and let me introduce you. . . . Oh, forget it! Jason is the shyest child on the face of the earth!" You can well imagine Jason soaking up all that negative information about himself.

This leads us to step two in the Belief Process. After children receive some information about themselves, they draw conclusions like I'm smart, I love school, I always have a positive attitude about things, I'm going to be the valedictorian of my class someday. Or conclusions like I'm dumb, I'm never going to make it through school, my parents have given up on me, I'm just a troublemaker, I'm shy.

In step three of the Belief Process, our kids, just like adults, look for evidence to support their conclusions. Just like adults, they tend to find evidence to support their own conclusions. Once they find evidence to support their conclusions, it becomes easier for them to interpret whatever additional evidence comes their way as supporting their existing conclusions. It is simply human nature to do so.

After drawing a conclusion and finding bits of evidence to back it up, they repeat it to themselves in their own minds over and over again. It's called self-talk. As time goes on and children are faced with circumstances similar to the ones that first led them to the conclusion, they tend to repeat the process all over again. The same conclusion is drawn, followed by several rounds of self-talk that reinforce the conclusion.

All that self-talk and all that evidence mix together until the conclusion solidifies into what is commonly known as a "solid belief." Then the child acts according to his belief(s) on a daily basis. He does so automatically. This is fine if it's a positive belief he's picked up about himself. But it's pretty sad and limiting if it's a negative belief.

Let me share with you a true story from my childhood that I think will put the process into perspective for you. When I was in the second grade, one of my favorite things to do was to draw. So I was very happy one Tuesday afternoon when the teacher said, "We're going to have art class now. You can take out your paper and draw anything you like."

I grew up in a very small dairy town in southwestern Wisconsin, a beautiful little town with 2,500 people in a beautiful little valley. I chose to draw some of the hills behind my house. I drew a couple of trees on those hills, a deer on one side and a rabbit on the other. I was very proud of this drawing, and I was hoping the teacher would come by and say something nice about it.

Sure enough, just as I was coloring everything in, she stopped right at my desk and picked up my paper. I was smiling from ear to ear as she said to the class, "Everyone, look at Larry's picture." Everyone looked up and she pointed to my drawing. In a teacherlike way, she said, "Now, you see these two lollipop trees that Larry's drawn? You see, he's still drawing baby pictures!" That was step one: I had some information about myself. Step two, I drew a conclusion from the information: I couldn't draw.

Do you suppose the teacher intended for me to conclude that I could not draw? No, most certainly not, but intentions have nothing to do with the Belief Process. Parents can wholeheartedly intend to help their children grow up with positive beliefs about themselves, but if they go about it in a negative way, they can actually do the opposite. We'll explore that idea in just a minute.

As for step three, I searched for evidence to support my conclusion. In other words, from then on when I would draw things, I would look at my work and say to myself, Yeah, the teacher is right. I really can't draw.

Step four resulted naturally from this process. After a while, my conclusion became a part of my self-talk. By the time I got into high school biology, where I was supposed to draw frogs and guts and worms and things like that, I refused to do it. I would instead do whatever it took to get someone else to do it for me.

I acted according to this belief until I was thirty-five years old, when I was in a bookstore one day with one of my daughters. She wanted a particular book on drawing, so I told her to bring it to me so I could take a look at it. I opened to the introduction and in big bold print it said, "The definition of talent is practice." Immediately I thought to myself, Everybody knows you're either born with a talent or not. What's this practice stuff?

We took that book home and started practicing drawing together. After a couple of months, I was drawing again and loving it. After a couple of years, I even started drawing charcoal portraits of people.

It's a very interesting thing as an adult to come upon a negative belief that you thought was true about yourself, only to find out that it's not. It's almost shocking, actually, because people think of the beliefs they have about themselves as the way they were born; as the way God made them, if you will. To find out that beliefs are just made out of information and born of conclusions drawn using the immature reasoning of children gives a person a totally different perspective on both his own beliefs and on how children pick up beliefs about themselves.

Before we discuss how you can use this information to make sure your kids grow up with the kinds of beliefs you want them to grow up with, I want to mention a negative theory of parenting that many people learned from their parents. Their parents used this theory with the best of intentions, but it had a very negative impact on many of us as we were growing up, and it continues to negatively affect many children growing up today as their parents use it with them.

The theory operates like this. A parent decides he wants to raise his kids to be good people. To do so, he decides that the best thing he can do as a parent is to point out to his children what their faults are, so they can correct their faults and grow up to be better people. Let's say, for example, that I want my sixteen-year-old son to grow up to be a hard-working, responsible young man. Let's also say that it's Friday and my son has been calling me at work all day long, begging to use the car tonight because he's got a hot date. Finally, when I get home, I say, "Well, son, you can use the car tonight, but what about all of those chores you promised me you were going to do this weekend? Are you going to do them?"

My son, being the smart young man that he is, replies, "Sure, Dad!"

Satisfied, I agree to let him use the car.

Now let's say it's eleven o'clock on Sunday night, my son is heading for bed, and I call him aside and say, "Son, did you do your chores this weekend?"

My son replies, "I tried, Dad, but I just didn't have time. I'll do them tomorrow."

Exasperated, I respond, "You tried? You tried? Now let's be honest here—you didn't do squat around here this weekend. Not one thing. I didn't say anything to you about it, though, because I wanted to find out if I was right about you. And unfortunately I was. You know what your problem is, son? Your problem is you're just plain lazy. You're lazy, you're irresponsible, and, I hate to tell you this about yourself, but if you don't shape up, you're never going to amount to anything!"

Why would a parent approach a child in such a condemning fashion? One reason is that the parent learned it from his parents' generation, which got it from their parents' generation. The logic of this approach is, "Since my son has no insight of his own, someone has to point his faults out to him. Doesn't that duty fall on me, as his parent? Why am I being harsh with him? Not because I don't love him. No, I love him a hundred percent; he's my son. I'm being harsh with him in order to *motivate* him to change. I'm providing insight and motivation."

Providing a child with insight and motivation would seem to be a good thing for a parent to do. Unfortunately, when it is done through harsh and critical comments, the parent's worst fears may come to pass:

if a parent tells a child often enough that he's lazy and irresponsible, he will likely believe it and act accordingly.

Criticism is the number one strategy used in American families by parents to motivate their children to change. Criticism is also, by the way, the number one strategy people use in every kind of relationship in order to motivate other people to change, including parent to child, teacher to student, spouse to spouse, friend to friend, and employer to employee.

I find this of great interest, because if there's one thing people know about themselves, it's that they do not like it when someone criticizes them. Think about it for a moment. Recall the last time someone criticized you. Most likely you did not go to bed that night thinking, I think I'll get up tomorrow morning and write that person a thank-you note for that criticism! You probably felt angry and resentful. And, if you are like most people, it probably made you highly critical of the person who was criticizing you.

Parents cannot afford this cycle of criticism, because criticism destroys relationships. Human beings will not stay in a positive relationship with someone who is always criticizing us. Instead, we will do one of two things. Either we will try to get away from that person or, if we cannot get away from the critical person, we will dig in our heels and refuse to cooperate. We will even try to make that person as miserable as he has made us with that criticism.

Further, parents cannot afford this cycle of criticism in their families because there are millions of American parents today who have caustic relationships with their teenagers—often caused by the well-intended use of criticism. But there is good news. There are also millions of American parents who have great relationships with their teenagers. They will say to you, "Oh, we have a great time together. We talk all the time and do all kinds of things together as a family. My kids tell me about their problems and ask for advice." All parents, of course, want to count themselves in this group.

HERE'S HOW

Let me explain a very powerful process that will help you do just that. You can use this same process for three different purposes. First, you can use it to make sure your children grow up with positive beliefs about themselves. Second, you can use it to establish and maintain a positive relationship with your children as they grow up. Third, you can use it to heal a negative relationship with a child, now or in the future.

The first step of this process involves a little brainstorming. On a sheet of paper, write down all of the positive characteristics you want your children to grow up believing to be true about themselves. As examples, here is my list of the top twenty positive characteristics *I* want *my* kids to grow up believing to be true about themselves.

Positive Traits I Want My Kids to Believe They Have

Reliable
Respectful
Honest
Kind
Good manners
Positive attitude
Persistent
Good at making friends
Resourceful
Loving
Punctual
Good memory
Good at following directions
Creative
Patient
Hard worker
Enthusiastic
Good listener
Tolerant
Ambitious

Now let's suppose that every positive thing on this list is true about each of your children. I think it is true. In fact, I *know* it is true, because that's the way our children are born. As human beings, they are born with the seeds of every positive characteristic within them. However, the potential for the opposite, negative sides of these same characteristics lies within each child as well. That is simply the way they are born—with the potential to develop both good and bad characteristics.

The degree to which children grow up believing in their positive characteristics has a lot to do with the information they get from their parents as they grow up.

THE THREE-STEP BELIEF PROCESS

Once you have made your own list of the characteristics you want your children to know are true about themselves, pick three to focus on initially in the process I'll describe below.

As an example, let's use the qualities hardworking and responsible. These are good characteristics, because children who grow up with them will likely have a much higher quality of life than those who do not.

In the earlier scenario, I described how a parent may commonly try to instill these same qualities through criticism. But while children may push your buttons and tempt you down that road of trying to get to the positive through the negative, it will never work. There is only one thing at the end of that road, and it's a bad relationship with your child. Do not let yourself be fooled. *You can never, ever get to the positive through the negative.*

So if I want my son to grow up to be hardworking and responsible, I am going to have to find another strategy. First, I want to point out that I'm not going to let my son get away with not doing his chores. I've got to have some rules and consequences to motivate him to do them. That's what the Smart Discipline System is designed to do.

But there is another side to discipline, and that is encouraging positive behavior through instilling positive beliefs in your children. So, in our example, the first thing I'm going to do is look for any little bit of evidence I can find that my son is a hardworking, responsible young man. I say look for a little bit of evidence, because if you look for a lot of evidence, you will never find it and you will never get to step two. That won't do either your child or you any good.

In the first step of the process, then, I'll look for a little bit of evidence that he's a hardworking, responsible young man. Let's say I go away on a business trip one weekend. When I come home my wife says to me, "You know, this weekend our son did all the chores you left for him to do. I also needed him to do a bunch of other stuff, and he did that, too. He worked hard and did a good job." Having this information, I have a little bit of evidence that he is hardworking and responsible.

When my son is heading for bed at eleven o'clock on Sunday night, I call him aside and say, "Son, your mother told me when I got home how hard you worked on getting your chores done. She tells me you also did a bunch of other stuff for her. This tells me you're a hardworking, responsible young man, and I appreciate that about you."

With these few simple sentences, I have completed a powerful three-step process. First, I pointed out to my son some positive evidence that this characteristic was true about him. It is crucial to point out the evidence, because if you don't attach the characteristic to evidence, what you are saying will be either disregarded or discounted by your child.

Second, I labeled him with a positive characteristic. I told him, "This tells me you're a hardworking, responsible young man . . ." By telling him directly that a positive characteristic is true about him, I am helping him script some positive self-talk.

Third, I told him I appreciated that about him: "You did all the chores. That tells me you're a hardworking, responsible young man, and *I appreciate that about you.*"

Here is another example. I'm having trouble with one of my daughters being late. The first thing I do is look for an example of her being on time. Let's say her mother tells her to get home from cheerleading practice by six o'clock for supper. This particular evening I notice she is not only on time, but she shows up early and helps her mother set the table and get supper ready. So, later that night when she is heading for bed, I might say something like "I heard your mother ask you to be home by six tonight for supper. Not only did you get home on time, but you came early and helped your mother get supper on the table. That tells me you are not only a punctual person, but considerate and helpful as well. I really appreciate that about you."

This process is magic! It's magic because one of the best things I know about being a parent is that sometimes you can tell a child something positive about him *one time* and he'll believe you for a lifetime.

That's pretty wonderful, isn't it? It is especially wonderful when you think of all the opportunities there are to point out positive qualities about our kids. Regardless of a child's behavior, there are always positive things you can focus on.

Better yet, this process comes with a guarantee. If you point out the evidence of a positive quality to your child three or four times, there is only one thing that can happen: He'll go out into the world to prove that he does indeed have that quality.

Since I pointed out to my son that he was a hardworking and responsible young man, he is likely to look for evidence that it is true. It may well happen that at his after-school job he'll put in a bit of extra effort. He feels good about his efforts and makes the self-assessment "I am hardworking and responsible." As an added bonus, his hard work may be noticed and pointed out by his boss, further reinforcing the belief.

In the case of my daughter, she might make a special effort the next night to be home on time for supper again. Her mother may well express some appreciation for this. Feeling good about being on time, our daughter may start a habit of being on time in other areas of her life. As she does, it is certain that her self-talk will develop into a positive conclusion that she is a punctual person.

THREE WAYS TO BRING OUT THE BEST IN YOUR CHILDREN

This is a powerful process, and it works extremely well. Every time you make the effort to relay positive information and conclusions to your children, you will both build a positive relationship with your child and instill in her positive beliefs. Here are several ways you can start using the Belief Process to help instill positive beliefs in your children.

First, it is always powerful to communicate positive things to children one-on-one. Private communications with children are special to them. Doing so anytime is fine, but just before bed is especially good. As your child is going to sleep, you can bet that he will be repeating your words over and over in his mind. When he wakes your words will again come to mind and he will enthusiastically look forward to acting out the positive quality that day.

A second powerful way to communicate positive information to your children is to speak about it to someone else within their ear-shot. One way my wife and I did this was by standing beneath the air-conditioning vents in the kitchen so that when the kids were upstairs in their rooms, they were likely to hear us—especially if we spoke of them by name. One of us would say something like "Amanda was so kind to the little boy next door who's been home sick. I was really proud of her. She helped him with his math homework, and she helped him catch up on his science project. She's just a really caring young lady, isn't she? I really appreciate that about her." When children hear information about themselves surreptitiously, they absorb it like sponges and immediately internalize it. They accept it as true and act in ways to offer further evidence of its validity.

The third way is my favorite way of using the Belief Process for the benefit of children. You wait until your children go to bed, then get out a pencil and a piece of paper and write out the information. For example, "Dear Son: Today when I asked you about the trouble you got into at school, you told me the truth about it. I spoke with your teacher and she told me that you had owned up to exactly what you had done. Even though you knew you would get into trouble, you told the truth anyway. That tells me that you are an honest young man. I very much appreciate that about you. Love, Dad."

You tape the note on the bathroom mirror or in another place where he's going to find it first thing in the morning. Do you know what's going to happen to those notes? They will disappear. Most likely you will never see them again. Where are they going to disappear to? Straight into your child's heart! And from there they will never, ever disappear.

These kinds of things are absolutely wonderful to do with your children. Each time you use the Belief Process, you not only instill positive beliefs in your children, but you build your relationship with them as well. One day, these relationship will be stronger than steel. Although they might bend, they will never break.

As powerful as the Belief Process is, it can be difficult to put into practice. There are several reasons for this. One is that, as some parents say to me, "Hey, wait a minute! I've read articles lately that warn about the very thing you're talking about. They say that if you praise your child all the time, it'll just go to their heads. It will give them a bloated ego, and that's not a good thing at all!"

Let's think about this for a moment. When you grew up, did you get too much praise? I have asked this question to tens of thousands of people. Never has anyone told me that he did. Some say they got enough, but never has anyone said he got too much. I also ask people in my seminars if they know any failures who go around saying, "My problem is that my parents gave me too much praise when I was growing up!" In fact, people laugh at the absurdity of it.

At other times, parents say, "Now let's be fair here. I tried this stuff with my children and it doesn't work. I get positive with my kids and they just get negative back!" If that's what's happening in your family, it probably means a couple of things. First, you're probably raising teenagers! Second, it means these kids are saying to you in the only way they can, "Look, I think this is a bunch of garbage! I don't believe what you're saying, so I'm going to test you. I'm going to find out if you really mean it or not."

Children often test their parents. Frequently (and unfortunately), parents flunk these tests almost immediately. They get positive with their children; they get negative feedback; and then they dive right back into that swirling pool of negativity with their children. Children need their parents to pass the test by responding with something like "It's all right, son. I just wanted you to know." Then keep pointing out their positive behavior and corresponding characteristics. I promise you that if you do this, regardless of the negativity your children express, a small voice in the back of their minds will be saying, *Really? Maybe I am honest [kind, caring, hardworking, responsible . . .].* If you take the time and effort to repeat the Belief Process with them, focusing on any one positive trait, the payoff will most certainly come in their acting out that trait more often.

After one seminar, a woman came up to me excitedly and said, "I can hardly wait to try this stuff with my grandchildren! It's going to be powerful! It's going to be wonderful in their lives! But it's too bad it won't work with my fifteen-year-old daughter."

A bit taken aback, I replied, "Why would it be so powerful for your grandchildren, but not for your own daughter?"

She went on to explain that while all of those positive traits on my top twenty list were true about her grandchildren, none were true of her daughter (this daughter, by the way, was not the mother of any of the grandchildren). She claimed that while she hated to admit it, it was clear that her youngest daughter exhibited the opposite of these traits.

This parent was describing a common phenomenon that blinds many parents to the fact that all positive traits are true about every child. If a child's behavior becomes predominantly negative and the child continues to misbehave regardless of her parents' efforts to correct her, the parent often becomes hypersensitive to the child's negative behavior and desensitized to any of the child's positive behaviors. The result is that the parent complains constantly to the child about negative behavior while ignoring her positive behavior. Without intending for it to happen, both parent and child get locked into a pattern. The more criticism the parent metes out, the more the child misbehaves, which in turn is met with more parental criticism.

The only way out of this destructive pattern is for the parent to put a halt to the criticism. The parent must start looking for small examples of positive behavior and focusing on those. To correct the misbehavior, the Smart Discipline System can be used. However, the other side of discipline is getting children to *want to behave*. This is very important and can best be achieved by actively using the Belief Process.

PROOF POSITIVE

As I do for the participants of my Smart Discipline seminars, let me prove to you that the Belief Process will work 100 percent of the time for 100 percent of your children. To do that, let's take a brief trip down memory lane. Remember the time when you taught your children how to talk and how to walk? Those are the two most difficult things you will ever teach your children. Still, you taught them while they were just babies.

How did you do teach them? Most likely, you did it just like every other parent: through the use of 100 percent encouragement and praise. Never did it occur to you to say something like "Oh, Johnny, that's the tenth time you fell down today! You might as well give it up—you're never going to learn to walk!" Nor did you teach your children how to talk by saying, "By the way, it's not Dada. It's Daddy! Can't you get it right?"

No, you didn't do that. Instead you looked for any little bits of evidence that your child was headed in the right direction and pointed them out: "Oh, Johnny, Johnny, that's your first step! Take another one, son. That's it. Oh, you're walking, son! Come to Daddy. Mom, call Grandma and Grandpa! Call everybody over here to come watch. Johnny's walking!" When your child said, "Dada," you probably said, "Daddy? Well, here I am! Daddy's here." You probably did these kinds of things even though you don't see yourself as one of those "really positive" people.

The interesting thing is this. Even among people who don't think of themselves as being filled with enthusiasm, when they are teaching their children how to talk and walk, they have a core of positive energy that naturally flows out to their children. I like to point this out to people and say, "Maybe you haven't used up all of this positive energy. Maybe you still have enough of it left to point out to your children that they have some wonderful and positive traits so they can include them in their identities as they are growing up." Lucky, even blessed, are the children who have parents who take the time and effort to point out that these very positive characteristics are true about themselves!

10

Identifying Your
Children's Centers of Brilliance

In this chapter, you'll find some of the most important information a parent could ever want. It can be used to give a child one of the greatest gifts a parent can give: a belief that says, "I have what it takes to be successful in life."

Children who grow up with such a belief have a positive vision for their future that becomes their guiding light. From my work with over one hundred thousand kids around the United States, I have come to know firsthand the difference between children who have this positive vision for their future and those who don't. Kids who have an explicit view of their talents and how they will use them to be successful in life make healthy and productive choices. They are not as likely to get involved in drugs and other illicit behaviors. Why? Because they tend to make choices that will move them toward their vision of the future and stay away from behaviors that might inhibit their chances for success.

Young people who lack this positive belief that they have what it takes to be successful tend not to care about the future. They tend to make decisions based on what feels good at the moment or on what their friends are doing. The potential consequences of their decisions are of little importance because they don't view themselves as having anything to lose. You know who these teenagers are. They are the ones with an "I don't care" attitude who act accordingly.

As parents, we want to do whatever we can to make sure our children grow up with the beliefs that will enable them to be happy and successful in life. This chapter will help you do exactly that. You will discover what your children's talents are and how to help them to know both that they have unique capabilities and that they will be able to use them successfully.

More than that, I will help you show your children that they truly have a "center of brilliance," something that is unique and special about them. It says, "There is something wonderful about me, something that I can use to navigate through life not only to get the things I want, but to be of good use to others in my world."

Unfortunately, most people grow up thinking that they are only average or even less than average. It is easy for people to see that others have wonderful talents but think that their own talents, if they have any at all, are of little significance. This is too bad, especially because it is not true. Every human being has specific talents that can be developed far beyond the current norm. This is hard for most of us to believe. We think that only a chosen few have wonderful talents and that most of us are blessed with only modest talents at best.

Not so! All of us, including our children, have wonderful talents. I describe them as being our "centers of brilliance" to signify that each of us has within us explicit and wonderful capabilities. If we can help our children discover their "center of brilliance" and establish a solid belief that they have what it takes to be successful in life, we will give them a gift they will treasure their whole lives, as well as a positive vision for their future that will help guide them to make better choices for themselves as they grow up.

Because children most often adopt the same personal belief system as their parents, I have included instructions for adults to identify their own "centers of brilliance." Yes, even you have one. The tougher it is for you to believe this about yourself, the more you need to concentrate on finding and developing it. Once you find your center of brilliance, you will do a great service to both yourself and your children. You will be happier, perhaps wealthier, of greater service to people in the world, and a more positive role model for your children. For these reasons, I highly recommend that everyone focus their energies on discovering and developing their own "center of brilliance."

WHY IT'S SO IMPORTANT TO FIND YOUR CHILDREN'S CENTERS OF BRILLIANCE

Some people have talents that, from the time they are very young, are easily identifiable to all those around them. Often, these are the children who excel in art, music, acting, or athletics. Also—and this is important—their behavior is normally exemplary.

These children learn early that they have a center of brilliance within them that they can use to be successful in life. Even more than that, they know firsthand how wonderful it feels when they use their center of brilliance.

When you're engaged in activities utilizing your center of brilliance, time and problems melt away and you are aware of neither. Your whole mind, body, and soul become completely immersed in what you are doing. As an added bonus, your body releases endorphins into your bloodstream to produce what many know as the "runner's high." It's a great feeling.

Unfortunately, only a small percentage of people grow up knowing what their center of brilliance is. Of those who do, only a few actually pursue their natural talent for happiness and success. Instead, they go along with the well-meaning expectations of those around them, which can steer them into family businesses, "more stable" careers, or the pursuit of dreams their parents have for them to become doctors, dentists, lawyers, pastors, and the like.

We've all been told we have God-given talents. We even believe it for a while when we're young. But then life starts to take its toll. We get really excited about something, so we try it out. If we're not one of the fortunate few who have an exceptional talent in that area, one of the following is likely to happen to us:

1. *Mistakes.* We try something and make mistakes. Mistakes are frustrating and sometimes embarrassing; therefore, they can cause us to conclude that we don't have any worthwhile talent in that area. We quit, which protects us from further frustration or embarrassment.

2. *Criticism.* Our efforts at first are likely going to be less than perfect. When we do something less than perfectly, often someone will criticize us. This criticism might be given out of a desire to

help us or ridicule us. The intention, though, doesn't matter, because the typical human reaction to criticism of any type is emotional pain. To avoid further pain, we human beings tend to stop doing the thing that caused the pain.

3. *Comparisons.* When we start to do something new, it is only natural that we compare our results with those around us. Since we're new to the game, our results will likely seem poor compared to what others are producing. This can be discouraging and may cause us to conclude that we don't have any talent in that area. So we quit.

4. *Negative declarations.* Once in a while, when we are not long into developing a particular talent, we are unfortunate enough to encounter someone who decrees our results inadequate and who further predicts that there is no way we will be successful in this particular endeavor. We may agree and give up. Why? Because we tent to believe other people's judgments, especially those of people who we think know better than we do.

5. *Impatience.* Sometimes our progress in the development of a skill is painfully slow. If our pace clashes with an expectation that we were going to progress by leaps and bounds and that we would be the "best" in short order, we can start to feel like a failure. When we don't meet our own expectations on schedule, we may conclude that we are a failure and want to quit. If we do, we often conclude, "It's just as well I quit, because I don't have any talent for that anyway!"

As we grow up, we may have these experiences a number of times as we try different talents. The trouble is that as we start having these negative experiences that lead us to cross different talents off our lists, we may well cross off the very talent that was "God-given."

Having done so, we start searching for other ways to determine what we'll do when we grow up. The majority of us come to answer the question in one of several ways:

1. We ask around to find out what careers pay the most.
2. We do some research to find out what careers are going to be in greatest demand in the coming years.

3. We find out what our friends are going to do and see if that holds any appeal for us.
4. We go into the family business.
5. We follow our parents' expectations.
6. We look at the help wanted ads to see what kind of job we can get.

A few of us may take an aptitude test. However, most of us lay aside the results and pursue one of the aforementioned avenues to decide how we will spend the majority of our waking hours on this earth. This would be fine except for one thing: So many of us fail miserably and end up job-hopping. Or we spend years doing something we've become fairly good at but are miserable doing.

The consequences are the same. We end up wondering what's wrong with us. Despite our hard work, success and happiness continually elude us. It's depressing. This can affect us so much that we wake up every day feeling tired, crabby, and downhearted.

Does this sound familiar? If so, you are not alone. Millions of Americans today are living lives of frustration and dissatisfaction. But now for the good news. You have a center of brilliance within you! You can find it, *and* you can develop it. Once you start using it daily, your discontent with life will give way to happiness and contentment. Life will cease to be a struggle. You will no longer need to seek opportunity. Opportunity will come to you.

If this isn't enough, here are eight other reasons why it is so important to discover and develop your center of brilliance.

1. **Your persistence will greatly improve.** Whenever you set your sights on achieving anything worthwhile, problems *will* crop up. When we encounter problems, we tend to quit. If you are pursuing something you really feel good about, there is a much better chance that you will find a way to solve the problem and continue. This is of tantamount importance, because persistence is absolutely necessary if you want to progress in life.
2. **You will be much more motivated.** One of the biggest obstacles to achievement of one's goals is inertia. Once we get started, we do fine. But we have to begin again every day, some-

times several times per day. This is tough, especially when the going gets tough. If you are in pursuit of developing your center of brilliance, starting is easier. Your natural enthusiasm for the task at hand will motivate you the more you spend time using your center of brilliance.

3. **You will be more focused.** Maintaining the focus necessary for success is often difficult. In any given year, several opportunities may be presented to us. They may be lucrative opportunities presented by highly persuasive people. If your goals are aligned with your center of brilliance, you have a way to decide whether to divert some of your time and energy to the opportunity. If it is one in which you would be using your center of brilliance and which would help you reach your goals, then go for it. If not, decline it politely and confidently go about your business.

4. **Your skills will improve constantly.** When you are engaged in using your center of brilliance, you will be constantly motivated to improve. You will do what is necessary to practice, and so evolve. In his best-selling book *Emotional Intelligence,* Daniel Goleman says that it takes on average ten years to become an expert at anything. During those ten years, if you focus on improving every day, success, happiness, and the money you desire will start to flow in greater and greater measure. After those ten years, you will be an expert. Once this happens, life is no longer a struggle. Money, success, and happiness become a way of living.

5. **You will be willing to take on new challenges.** When we are spending our lives doing things we don't really care for, we get lethargic. In our lethargy we steer clear of risks and challenges. Nothing seems worth the effort. We stop caring. "Good enough" becomes our standard of measure. Not so when you are engaged in the use of your center of brilliance. Each new challenge becomes something you look forward to. You don't want to avoid it even if the opportunity to do so presents itself. When you do meet the challenge successfully, you start looking for a bigger and better challenge.

6. **Your self-confidence will skyrocket.** You will use your talent to do things you never thought possible. You'll be surprised

at how well you do them. As a result, your self-confidence will grow by leaps and bounds. Just as the "rich get richer," the self-confident get more self-confident.

7. **Your energy level will increase.** When we are bored with our lives, depressed, or feel like failures, our energy level sinks. It can get so low that we can sleep ten hours and still feel tired. When you are developing and using your center of brilliance, energy is released. You sleep less and pop out of bed in the morning. You don't have to force it. It just happens naturally. You start to feel and act enthusiastically.

8. **Your relationships will improve.** The more you develop and use your center of brilliance, the higher your levels of happiness and satisfaction with your life. As an added bonus, your relationships will improve dramatically, because you no longer look to others for your happiness. Instead, your new enthusiasm for life spills over and affects everyone around you. You become more likable, more positive, and more energetic. In short, you go from being a needy person to one willing and able to fill the needs of others.

For all of these reasons, it is important to help your children discover their center(s) of brilliance. By doing so you will be helping them to

- become more persistent;
- be more motivated;
- stay focused;
- improve their skills;
- take on new challenges;
- increase their self-confidence;
- be more energetic; and
- develop healthy social and love relationships.

In short, knowing that you have a center of brilliance and identifying it is a really good idea for both you and your children. Those armed with this information have a much better shot at success and happiness in school, careers, and relationships.

THE SEVEN CENTERS OF BRILLIANCE

Harvard researcher Dr. Howard Gardner has become well-known for his studies of human intelligence. He has identified seven areas of intelligence and found that every human being has at least one of these. Further, he points out that each of these can be developed and used to help a person lead a happy and productive live.

The following categories are based on the seven areas of intelligence. I have denoted these categories as "centers of brilliance." They reflect my personal belief that every man, woman, and child is much smarter than he or she ever imagined.

PEOPLE BRILLIANCE

People who are gifted in this area do well at working with people. They have a unique ability to perceive the moods, intentions, emotions, personalities, motivations, and desires of other people. Those whose brilliance lie in this area are happiest and excel the most while doing the following: empathizing, tutoring, counseling, selling, coaching, coordinating activities, assessing others, teaching, leading seminars, persuading, motivating, recruiting, inspiring, encouraging, supervising, collaborating, leading teams, negotiating, mentoring, and publicizing.

Typical professions include school principal, teacher, human resources worker, social worker, salesperson, travel agent, nurse, arbitrator, public relations worker, social director, anthropologist, politician, psychologist, seminar leader, entrepreneur, or negotiator.

BODY BRILLIANCE

People who are gifted in this area do well at using their bodies. They are skillful at physical movements, handling objects, and hand-eye coordination. They are happiest and excel the most while doing the following: organizing or playing sports, modeling clothes, acting or performing, installing, repairing, restoring, woodworking, building, miming, dancing, manufacturing, delivering, and working outside.

Typical professions include professional athlete, coach, physical education teacher, physical therapist, massage therapist, surgeon or physician, dancer, actor, model, jeweler, mechanic, farmer, factory worker, carpenter, craftsperson, choreographer, recreational leader, or forest ranger.

WORD BRILLIANCE

People gifted in this area do well at working with words. They have a unique ability to negotiate, entertain, instruct, and write. Those whose brilliance lie in this area are happiest and excel when engaged in writing, teaching, lecturing, debating, negotiating, listening, giving instructions, telling stories, proofreading, word processing, reporting, editing, and speaking foreign languages.

Typical professions include writer, journalist, lawyer, secretary, English teacher, announcer, speech pathologist, translator, editor, curator, librarian, or legal assistant.

EMOTIONAL AND SPIRITUAL BRILLIANCE

People with talents in this area are good at knowing the inner self, both their own and that of others. They excel in spiritual and philosophical thought, are introspective, and are tuned in to the feelings of those around them. Those whose center of brilliance lies in this area are happiest and excel the most when engaged in counseling, helping others, writing, planning and organizing, problem solving, setting goals, meditating, discerning opportunities, appraising or evaluating, and working alone.

Typical professions include minister, psychologist, therapist, program planner, counselor, social worker, entrepreneur, seminar leader, or teacher of philosophy, psychology, or religion.

MUSICAL BRILLIANCE

People gifted in this area are good at producing rhythms and melodies, are said to have a "good ear," can keep time, can sing and/or play musical instruments, and can listen to music with discernment. Those whose center of brilliance is musical are happiest and excel when engaged in singing, playing instruments, composing, arranging music, conducting, teaching music, directing, listening to music, analyzing and evaluating music, and transcribing music.

Typical professions include Conductor, music teacher, disc jockey, piano tuner, songwriter, band member or leader, music therapist, studio engineer, choral director, singer, instrument inventor or maker.

VISUAL AND SPATIAL BRILLIANCE

People gifted in this area are good at transforming ideas into pictures and at conceptualizing three-dimensional space. Those whose center of brilliance is in this area are happiest and excel when engaged in designing, inventing, mapping, navigating, photographing, decorating, drafting, illustrating, drawing, painting, teaching art, choreographing, creating advertisements or visual presentations, filming, or visualizing.

Typical professions include architect, inventor, choreographer, pilot, navigator, sculptor, interior decorator, graphic artist, advertising agency owner, surveyor, engineer, photographer, art teacher, or fine artist.

LOGICAL BRILLIANCE

People gifted in this area are good at working with numbers, matters of logic, creating hypotheses, thinking in terms of cause and effect, and patterns or concepts. Those whose center of brilliance lies in this area are happiest and excel when engaged in calculating, hypothesizing, computing, working with computers or computer programs, using statistics, reasoning, estimating, auditing, accounting, systematizing, doing research, working with economic theory, and budgeting.

Typical professions include underwriter, economist, banker, science teacher, bookkeeper, accountant, purchasing agent, computer analyst, mathematician, scientist, statistician, librarian, auditor, or financial analyst.

You may well have identified one, two, or even several areas you or your children fit into. You will have an even better idea after you take and score the center of brilliance inventories. There is one version for adults and one version you'll fill out for your children. You may want to photocopy enough inventories and scoring sheets to have a separate one for each child.

THE CENTER OF BRILLIANCE INVENTORY FOR CHILDREN

These questions will help stimulate your thoughts about your children's centers of brilliance. Respond to the inventory statements as honestly and as quickly as you can. Don't ponder any question for long or change your answers. Your initial "gut" response is most likely to be the most accurate response. Avoid scoring your answers as 1s or 6s except when you feel strongly one way or the other. If you don't know the answer to a statement pertaining to your child, and you can't find it out, then score the answer as a 3.

INSTRUCTIONS

Rate each of the next fifty-six items according to how true that item is for your child by assigning a number from 1 to 6. For example, if the statement is "This child enjoys working with numbers," you would choose your rating as follows:

> "6" if the statement describes your child all of the time or is clearly true.
> "4" or "5" if the statement is often true.
> "3" if the statement is true half of the time or if you don't know the answer.
> "2" if the statement is true once in a while.
> "1" if the statement is clearly not true about your child.

_____ 1. This child loves to read.
_____ 2. The child likes to play with chemistry sets or do science projects.
_____ 3. This child frequently daydreams.
_____ 4. Lots of physical activity is a must for this child.
_____ 5. Music is a major part of this child's enjoyment in life.

_____ 6. Striking up a conversation with a stranger is not a problem for this child.

_____ 7. This child is quite self-reliant and independent.

_____ 8. This child really enjoys writing poems or stories.

_____ 9. This child picks up math concepts quickly and easily.

_____ 10. This child loves to draw.

_____ 11. This child loves being outside more than anything else.

_____ 12. This child always seems to be either singing something or humming a tune.

_____ 13. Helping to settle arguments between people is one thing this child is good at.

_____ 14. This child is always working on a project or hobby alone.

_____ 15. Bookstores and libraries are two of this child's favorite places to spend time.

_____ 16. Puzzles and brainteasers are enjoyable for this child.

_____ 17. This child can look at the clouds and easily discern pictures and patterns.

_____ 18. Playing organized sports is this child's idea of fun.

_____ 19. Playing Name That Tune is something this child would be good at.

_____ 20. People tell me that this child is "good with people."

_____ 21. Meditation will probably appeal to this child one day.

_____ 22. Word games like Password and Scrabble are games at which this child excels.

_____ 23. This child is forever seeking out the patterns and sequences in things.

_____ 24. This child found (or would find) geometry more interesting than algebra.

_____ 25. People tell me that this child is well coordinated.

_____ 26. This child often makes up tunes and melodies.

_____ 27. People come to this child for advice or to talk out their problems.

_____ 28. This child often reads about real people and their lives.

_____ 29. In grade school, this child talked too much, according to the teacher.

_____ 30. This child likes to know how things work.

_____ 31. This child is great at picking out and coordinating colors.

_____ 32. This child loves to work with finger paints and clay.

_____ 33. This child perks up dramatically when music is being played.

_____ 34. This child always has an easy time making friends.

_____ 35. This child has a secret place to spend time alone.

_____ 36. I wouldn't be surprised if this child became a great writer.

_____ 37. Blocks, Tinker Toys, Legos, and Erector Sets are among this child's favorite toys.

_____ 38. This child is great at taking things apart and putting them back together.

_____ 39. This child loves to act out skits and/or be in plays.

_____ 40. This child loves to play musical instruments.

_____ 41. This child always seems to take leadership roles in groups and clubs.

_____ 42. This child frequently writes or talks about feelings and personal events.

_____ 43. This child has always had many favorite books.

_____ 44. This child loves science-related programs like *Wild Kingdom.*

_____ 45. This child likes to build castles made of cards and/or sand.

_____ 46. This child has special abilities in sports and/or sports-related activities.

_____ 47. People have always remarked upon this child's superior music abilities.

_____ 48. This child has an instinctive ability to pick up on how others are feeling.

_____ 49. This child is very interested in religious matters, activities, and written materials.

_____ 50. Memorizing stories, poems, and facts is something this child is very good at.

_____ 51. This child likes playing the role of a lawyer.

_____ 52. People tell me this child has an active imagination.

_____ 53. This child loves to play charades.

_____ 54. This child frequently talks about music.

_____ 55. A sense of compassion is the guiding force in this child's life.

_____ 56. From an early age, this child has always had an independent spirit.

Now go back and find the three statements you feel the most strongly about as they apply to your child. Add six points to each. Then transfer your scores to the score sheet and follow the instructions.

CENTER OF BRILLIANCE INVENTORY SCORING SHEET
FOR CHILDREN

Transfer your answers to the blanks below (the numbers below correspond to the numbers of the questions you answered). Be sure to add an extra six points to each of the three items you feel the most strongly about.

Next, add each column and divide each by eight. The result represents how you see your child's seven center(s) of brilliance.

	Word Brilliance	Logical Brilliance	Picture and Spatial Brilliance
	1._____	2._____	3._____
	8._____	9._____	10._____
	15._____	16._____	17._____
	22._____	23._____	24._____
	29._____	30._____	31._____
	36._____	37._____	38._____
	43._____	44._____	45._____
	50._____	51._____	52._____
TOTAL:	_____	_____	_____
	÷8	÷8	÷8
AVERAGE:	_____	_____	_____

Body Brilliance	Musical Brilliance	People Brilliance	Emotional and Spiritual Brilliance
4._____	5._____	6._____	7._____
11._____	12._____	13._____	14._____
18._____	19._____	20._____	21._____
25._____	26._____	27._____	28._____
32._____	33._____	34._____	35._____
39._____	40._____	41._____	42._____
46._____	47._____	48._____	49._____
53._____	54._____	55._____	56._____
_____	_____	_____	_____
÷8	÷8	÷8	÷8
_____	_____	_____	_____

HOW TO HELP YOUR CHILDREN DISCOVER
(AND BELIEVE IN) THEIR CENTERS OF BRILLIANCE

Once you have scored the inventories for your children, you will want to use this information to help them come to know that they do indeed have centers of brilliance. Here are a few suggestions on how you can go about it:

1. Make a mental note of the three centers of brilliance in which you scored your child the highest.
2. Look for evidence that your child is doing well in these areas. For example, if your child scored high in people brilliance, start taking note of how well he interacts with other people. Notice specific behaviors.
3. (Using this same example) Point out to your child that you noticed how well he interacts with others. Describe specific things you have seen him do that leads you to think this (for example, "Jason, I saw you talking and making friends with the new boy at Sunday school today—you sure are good at making friends").
4. Predict to your child that he will one day use this talent to become successful in life (for example, "Everywhere you go, you seem to make friends easily, Jason. People who have a talent getting along with others often end up using that talent to be teachers, coaches, salespeople, and psychologists. I think you would do really well at any of those things").
5. Keep pointing out examples of your child's talents. The more you do, the better off your child will be and the stronger her positive vision for the future will be.
6. Do not be dissuaded by negative reactions from your child. If your child reacts negatively, she is telling you in the only way she knows how that she needs you to keep up the positive feedback. The more negatively she reacts, the more she needs you to stay your course!
7. Take any bit of positive information you can find and use it to affirm your child's talents and predict future success. Do not wait until you have overwhelming evidence, or you and your child will remain stuck on zero.

Remember that helping your child discover and develop his centers of brilliance is one of the best things you can do as a parent. It gives him a vision of his future filled with hope. This is truly a gift of love and will make a profound difference in his life.

THE CENTER OF BRILLIANCE INVENTORY FOR ADULTS

These questions will help stimulate your thoughts about your own centers of brilliance. By taking the time to answer and score the inventory, you should be able to pinpoint your center(s) of brilliance. This is important to know, as your children will be very curious to find out what your talents are when you start pointing out their talents—it's just the way children are.

Children like to compare themselves to their parents. Doing so helps them both to define themselves and to decide what is important. So be prepared to give an informed answer when your child asks you what your talents are. If you know, she will place emphasis on discovering her own talents as well.

To further assist you in defining your talents, additional questions follow the inventory.

Respond to the statements in the inventory as honestly and as quickly as you can. Don't ponder any statement for long or change your answers. Your initial "gut" response is most likely to be the most accurate response.

Avoid scoring your answers as 1s or 6s except when you feel strongly one way or the other. If you don't know the answer to a question pertaining to your childhood and can't find out, then score the answer as a 3.

INSTRUCTIONS

Rate each of the next fifty-six items according to how true that item is for you by assigning a number from 1 to 6. For example, if the statement is "I enjoy working with numbers," you would choose your rating as follows:

> "6" if the statement describes you all of the time or is clearly true about you.
> "4" or "5" if the statement is often true.
> "3" if the statement is about your childhood and you don't know the answer.

"2" or "3" if the statement is true once in a while.

"1" if the statement is clearly not true about you.

_____ 1. I love to read.

_____ 2. When I was a child I liked to play with chemistry sets or do science projects.

_____ 3. I frequently daydream.

_____ 4. Physical activity is a must for me.

_____ 5. Music is a major part of my enjoyment in life.

_____ 6. Striking up a conversation with a stranger is not a problem for me.

_____ 7. I am quite self-reliant and independent.

_____ 8. When I was a child I liked to write poems or stories.

_____ 9. I pick up math concepts quickly and easily.

_____ 10. When I was growing up I loved to draw.

_____ 11. I love being outside. It doesn't matter so much what I'm doing as long as I'm outside doing it.

_____ 12. I always seem to be either singing something or humming a tune to myself.

_____ 13. Helping to settle arguments between people is one thing I am good at doing.

_____ 14. When I was a child I always had a project or hobby I was working on by myself.

_____ 15. Bookstores and libraries are two of my favorite places to spend time.

_____ 16. Puzzles and brainteasers are enjoyable, and I do them frequently.

_____ 17. I can look at the clouds and easily discern pictures and patterns.

_____ 18. Coaching and/or playing organized sports is my idea of fun.

_____ 19. Playing Name That Tune is something I am good at.

_____ 20. People tell me that I am "good with people."

_____ 21. Meditation appeals to me.

_____ 22. Word games like Password and Scrabble are games I excel at.

_____ 23. My mind automatically seeks out patterns and sequences in things.

_____ 24. Geometry is more interesting than algebra.

_____ 25. People tell me that I am well coordinated.

_____ 26. I often make up tunes and melodies.

_____ 27. People come to me for advice or to talk out their problems.

_____ 28. I often read self-help books.

_____ 29. In grade school I was told I talked too much.

_____ 30. I like to know how things work.

_____ 31. I am great at picking out and coordinating colors.

_____ 32. When I was a child I loved to work with finger paints and clay.

_____ 33. I use music to help perk myself up.

_____ 34. I have always had an easy time making friends.

_____ 35. As a child, I had a secret place all my own.

_____ 36. There is a book inside of me screaming to get out.

_____ 37. Blocks, Tinker Toys, Legos, and Erector Sets were among my favorite toys as a child.

_____ 38. I am great at taking things apart and putting them back together.

_____ 39. As a child, I loved to act out skits and be in plays.

_____ 40. As a child, I loved to play musical instruments.

_____ 41. As a child, I took leadership roles in groups and clubs.

_____ 42. As a child, I frequently wrote or talked about my feelings and the events in my life.

_____ 43. As a child, I had many favorite books.

_____ 44. As a child, I loved science-related programs like *Wild Kingdom* and *Mr. Wizard.*

_____ 45. As a child, I loved to build castles made of cards and/or sand.

_____ 46. I have special abilities in sports and/or sports-related activities.

_____ 47. People have always made remarks about my superior music abilities.

_____ 48. I have an instinctive ability to pick up on how others are feeling.

_____ 49. I am very interested in religious matters, activities, and written materials.

_____ 50. Memorizing stories, poems, and facts was something I was especially good at in school.

_____ 51. I like playing devil's advocate.

_____ 52. People tell me I have a creative imagination.

_____ 53. I love to play charades.

_____ 54. I frequently talk to my friends about music.

_____ 55. My sense of compassion is a guiding force in my life.

_____ 56. From an early age, I have had an independent spirit.

Now go back and find the three statements you feel the most positive about. Add six points to each of these. Then transfer your scores to the score sheet.

CENTER OF BRILLIANCE INVENTORY
FOR ADULTS SCORING SHEET

Transfer your answers to the blanks below (the numbers below correspond to the numbers of the questions you answered). Be sure to add in an extra six points to each of the three items that you feel the most strongly about.

Next, add each column and divide each by eight. The result represents how you see yourself in relation to your seven center(s) of brilliance.

	Word Brilliance	Logical Brilliance	Picture and Spatial Brilliance
	1._____	2._____	3._____
	8._____	9._____	10._____
	15._____	16._____	17._____
	22._____	23._____	24._____
	29._____	30._____	31._____
	36._____	37._____	38._____
	43._____	44._____	45._____
	50._____	51._____	52._____
TOTAL:	_____	_____	_____
	÷8	÷8	÷8
AVERAGE:	_____	_____	_____

Body Brilliance	Musical Brilliance	People Brilliance	Emotional and Spiritual Brilliance
4._____	5._____	6._____	7._____
11._____	12._____	13._____	14._____
18._____	19._____	20._____	21._____
25._____	26._____	27._____	28._____
32._____	33._____	34._____	35._____
39._____	40._____	41._____	42._____
46._____	47._____	48._____	49._____
53._____	54._____	55._____	56._____
_____	_____	_____	_____
÷8	÷8	÷8	÷8
_____	_____	_____	_____

At this point you should have an excellent idea of what your centers of brilliance are. To give you an even better idea of your innate talents, I suggest taking the time to answer the questions below. For best results, write out your responses.

Look for patterns and common themes in your answers. By the end of the process, you should have a solid idea of exactly what to say when your child asks, "What are your centers of brilliance?"

1. When you finished high school, what was the first thing you did with your life?
   Why did you do this?
   Was it your idea or someone else's?
   If you went on to school, what did you major in?
   How do you feel about the choices you made now?

2. What vision did you have for your future when you were a young adult in relation to work?
   How did your first job fit into this vision?
   What did you like about your first job as an adult?
   What did you dislike about your first job as an adult?

3. What did you do next, and why did you make the change?
   What did you like and dislike about what you did next?

4. Continue analyzing the job changes you made, answering why you made the changes and what you liked and disliked about the work and work settings. Use extra sheets of paper to record your answers.

5. As you look back over your career so far, do you recognize any common themes or patterns?
   How do you feel about these patterns and themes?

6. As you look back over your career, were there times that you especially enjoyed?
   What was it that you enjoyed?

7. As you look back over your career, were there times you especially disliked?
   What was it about these times that you did not enjoy?

8. Have you ever turned down a promotion or job? If so, describe it.
   Why did you turn it down?

9. As you look to the future, what things would you like to avoid? Why?

10. What are your long-range career goals?
    What would your long-range goals be if you had no fears or limits?

11. As you look ahead, what are you looking forward to in your career? Why?

12. What do you think your next job will be? After that, what?

13. For you, what would be the "ultimate" job?

14. What do you think is most likely to happen over the next ten years in your career? Why?

15. How would you describe your career to others?

16. What do you especially like to do?

17. What are you best at doing?

18. What do you want most out of your work?

19. What motivates you most at work?

20. What hampers your work performance?

21. What insights have you come to in relation to what work setting fits you best?

22. What direction do you think would be best for you to take in your career?

23. If you were to be successful in taking this direction, would you have a high level of job satisfaction? If so, why? If not, what kind of job would make you happy?

   If you have completed these questions and the center of brilliance inventory for adults, you should have a very good idea of both your innate talents and what career setting would satisfy you the most. It is my contention that people who engage themselves in work that makes use of their innate talents and who work in a setting that fits their personality have an optimum chance of achieving success and happiness in life. They also are well positioned as good parental role models to help their children to do the same.

   Please note: While I do not suggest that people go out and make sudden wholesale changes in their lives, I strongly encourage people to explore work opportunities and settings that will bring out their best.

PART THREE

Smart Discipline Solutions to Homework and School Problems

11

Using Smart Discipline
to Correct Behavior Problems at School

One of the most uncomfortable things for a parent is to hear that his child is misbehaving at school. It's not only frustrating—it's embarrassing. Unfortunately, I know of what I speak. Having raised five children, I have been called to the school on numerous occasions to be confronted with some heinous behavior of which my children had been found guilty.

When one of my daughters was in the fourth grade, I knew after the first day of school we were in for a tough year. At supper that night she innocently asked, "Daddy, what does 'belligerent' mean?"

My inborn parental ability to divine trouble prompted me to ask, "Why do you ask, darling?"

" 'Cause that's what my teacher called me today!"

Like a good parent, I explained to her in no uncertain terms that she was not to be disrespectful to her teacher in any way. In fact, she had better toe the line because she was going to be in "big trouble" if I found out she was misbehaving. Her mother also threw in a few warnings about how children who misbehave at school end up flunking. If that happened, she would be held back and all her friends would go on to the fifth grade without her.

The very next week we got a note from the teacher. It informed us that our daughter was being disruptive in class, that she was being disrespectful, that her homework was a mess, and that we should take immediate action to fix the problem before she flunked the fourth grade.

This, as you might imagine, was both frustrating and embarrassing. Frustrating because we had done what we thought we should do to correct the situation, and embarrassing because we felt as if we were being accused of being negligent in our duties as parents.

Once past the emotions of the situation, we put together a plan of action. We decided to tie the behavior problems at school to the Smart Discipline System at home. So we created some reporting forms (see forms at the end of this chapter) and sat down with our daughter.

We explained to her that she was going to have to take a daily report to the teacher at the end of every school day for the next two weeks and ask her to fill it out, answering "yes" or "no" to three statements on the form. One states that schoolwork was done on time, one that schoolwork was done properly, and one that classroom behavior was acceptable. For each "no" the teacher checked, we explained, our daughter would get an X on her Smart Discipline chart at home. If she failed to bring a report home for any reason, she would automatically get three Xs on her chart.

She responded with a stream of indignant protests. "But Dad, that's not fair! None of the rest of the kids have to do this. If you make me do this, I'll be so embarrassed. Why do you always have to find ways to embarrass me? Besides, if you do this, I'll end up losing my bike privileges, and how will I get to school?"

To which my wife wisely and calmly responded, "Those are good questions and good points. However, we are going to do this anyway."

We then made an appointment with the teacher. Like most teachers, she was more than willing to cooperate because we didn't blame her for the problem. We showed her the Smart Discipline charts and the daily school reports. We explained that our daughter would face losing privileges at home if she misbehaved at school. Then we asked for her cooperation in filling out the daily reports. She said she would be happy to do this as long as it was our daughter's responsibility to bring one to her each day when school ended.

Even though this made a lot of sense to us, we worried about whether or not our daughter would comply and especially whether she would be teased by the other students. Fortunately, things turned out better than expected.

Our daughter brought a report home every single day. We were shocked, since her memory for school-related projects was notoriously bad. But in this case we didn't have to remind her. Even more surprising, her attitude about it was incredibly positive. She proudly showed us her reports each day, neatly completed with affirmative answers to the questions.

Best of all, though, was the complete change in her behavior at school. She literally became a model student. This was confirmed by the teacher on Friday of the second week. She wrote on the last daily report, "Your daughter is an absolute delight to have in my class!"

What a turnaround! We were so pleased. On reflection, we realized that we had set up our daughter for success. In other words, we had made it clear to her exactly what the rules were, what the consequences for breaking the rules would be, and our commitment to following through. Knowing these things made it easy for her to make the choice to change her behavior. Even after the two weeks were up, she continued to behave as though there were no doubt in her mind what would happen if she went back to misbehaving.

If your child is misbehaving at school and you would like to try this approach, here are the steps to follow.

> **Step 1:** If your child is in elementary school, photocopy a two-week supply of the daily school reports. If your child is older and has multiple teachers, photocopy a two-week supply of the weekly school reports.
>
> **Step 2:** Explain to your child that because of his or her misbehavior at school, it will be necessary to have the teacher(s) fill out the reports each day (or each week, for the older children). Explain that each "no" will result in an X and not bringing a report home will result in three Xs for daily reports or seven Xs for weekly reports.
>
> **Step 3:** Acknowledge objections and feelings. It is important to let your child know that you have heard his point of view and accept it. After doing so, reaffirm your commitment to following through.
>
> **Step 4:** Meet with your child's teacher(s). Show the teacher both the school reports you will need filled out and the Smart Discipline charts. Explain how your child will lose privileges at home for misbehavior at school. Ask if the teacher would be willing to complete the reports if your child is responsible for bringing them the report at the end of class. (Rarely will a teacher say no. If so, discuss the objections and ask the teacher for suggestions.)
>
> **Step 5:** Enjoy the results! Be sure to praise your child's good reports. And repeat the process until you are satisfied that the problem is corrected.

DAILY SCHOOL REPORT

Schoolwork was done on time   Yes _____ No _____
Schoolwork was done properly   Yes _____ No _____
Classroom behavior was acceptable   Yes _____ No _____
                    Comments:

_____

_____

_____

Teacher's Signature _____ Date _____

DAILY SCHOOL REPORT

Schoolwork was done on time   Yes _____ No _____
Schoolwork was done properly   Yes _____ No _____
Classroom behavior was acceptable   Yes _____ No _____
                    Comments:

_____

_____

_____

Teacher's Signature _____ Date _____

DAILY SCHOOL REPORT

Schoolwork was done on time   Yes _____ No _____
Schoolwork was done properly   Yes _____ No _____
Classroom behavior was acceptable   Yes _____ No _____
                    Comments:

_____

_____

_____

Teacher's Signature _____ Date _____

WEEKLY SCHOOL REPORT

Please answer "Yes" or "No" based on the following questions and sign. Chart is filled out based on performance for entire week.
>   A. Schoolwork was done on time
>   B. Schoolwork was done properly
>   C. Classroom behavior was acceptable

Subject	Teacher	Yes/No	Signature

WEEKLY SCHOOL REPORT

Please answer "Yes" or "No" based on the following questions and sign. Chart is filled out based on performance for entire week.
>   A. Schoolwork was done on time
>   B. Schoolwork was done properly
>   C. Classroom behavior was acceptable

Subject	Teacher	Yes/No	Signature

Three Effective
Homework Guidelines

My children's success in school is extremely important to me. If I am honest about it, part of the reason is that their level of success reflects on me as a parent. Our society seems to equate good grades with good parenting and bad grades with bad parenting.

Perhaps that's as it should be. When it comes down to it, our children need for us to care deeply about their success in school. Children whose parents care about success in school certainly have a better chance of caring about it themselves. Unfortunately, caring alone isn't always enough. Sometimes well-intended parental caring can result in constant hassles over school and homework. Whether you have these battles depends a lot on the child's attitude toward school.

Typically, children approach schoolwork in one of three ways. Some take to it like ducks to water. They love schoolwork and can't get enough of it. They can't wait until summer is over so they can go back to school. Lucky are the parents who have such children. They can look forward to years of good report cards and (by implication) high marks as parents.

Next are those children who view school and schoolwork as a necessary evil. They do it because they have to. Usually they would rather be doing something they consider more fun. But there are also times when they find their homework interesting, and at those times they really "get into it." Whether they are bored or interested determines how much prodding they will need to get their work done. The less often they are interested, the more often homework hassles are likely to occur.

Third, there are those who hate school. They will do anything and everything to avoid schoolwork. Parents of these children usually spend years hassling over school and homework. Some, for the sake of peace, eventually give up. When that happens, everyone loses.

Good news! Effective strategies exist to turn the tide. Attitudes toward homework and school can be changed. Homework hassles can be halted. And children can be motivated to do their best work on their own.

WHY HOMEWORK IS IMPORTANT

I think it's important to know just why homework is important for two reasons. First, so we can get our kids to understand its importance, since over time children (believe it or not) pick up on and adopt their parents' attitude that homework is a top priority. Second, we as parents need to be clear on the value of doing what our children need for us to do. This we especially need when our children are doggedly determined to fight us every step of the way. At these times we need every reason we can find to fight the urge to give up.

So let's look at the reasons why homework is so important.

Reason #1
There is a direct relationship between self-esteem and success in school. The more a child adopts the belief that he "has what it takes to be successful in school," the better he will do. Conversely, the more a child adopts the negative attitude that he "doesn't have what it takes to be successful in school," the worse he will do. Numerous studies over the last twenty-five years bear this out. As parents we know intuitively it is correct.

Homework plays an important role in the development of these beliefs because of the constant feedback a child gets about himself in relation to homework.

What I mean is this. As we've discussed in previous chapters, children adopt beliefs about themselves by listening for information. They listen to parents, relatives, teachers, and friends. When they hear something about themselves, they draw a conclusion and look for other evidence to determine if it is true or not. If a child finds this evidence, she starts to repeat the belief over and over again in her "self-talk" until it becomes a solid belief. Once it's a solid belief, she acts it out consistently and automatically.

The daily and most frequent feedback children get is in relation to homework. Parents see it. Teachers see it. Everyone evaluates it and makes comments to the child. From these comments, the child draws conclusions that boil down to either "I have what it takes to be successful in this subject" or the reverse.

The child then looks for further evidence to support her conclusions. Because she is seeking, she will usually find the evidence and end up adopting the conclusion as a belief.

If enough positive information is given to a child that her homework is done well, then the child concludes, "I have what it takes to be successful in school." Children who consistently get this feedback tend to love school and schoolwork.

On the other hand, if enough negative beliefs surrounding schoolwork are established, the child will likely conclude, "I don't have what it takes to be successful in school." These are the children who buck school, teachers, and homework all the way.

In summary, homework is important because of the daily feedback it provides to the child. If it is done correctly, neatly, and on time, all kinds of positive comments are made that lead to positive, productive beliefs. If it is done incorrectly, sloppily, or not at all, the reverse happens.

Reason #2

Time spent doing homework directly affects grades. You can almost predict the grades on your child's report card by the grades on his homework. In fact, teachers will tell you that a child at any level of academic achievement can improve his grades by concentration on homework. Educational studies show that students who consistently do homework outperform those who do not.

This is why I tell parents frustrated over poor report cards to stop harping on grades and change their focus to homework. Doing so can give both the parents and the child a handle on a solution. More on how to do this later.

Reason #3

Homework teaches responsibility and accountability. Lucky is the child who has a parent who conveys the message that she must take responsibility for doing her homework and, further, that she will be held accountable for it being done correctly, neatly, and on time.

Does this sound old-fashioned? If it does, I defend it on the basis of my belief that a child who grows up shouldering responsibility and accountability has a better chance at being successful in all aspects of life. Spiritually, emotionally, and mentally, she will simply do better. A child brought up in such a way, I assure you, will fare a lot better in her career and relationships as well.

Knowing most of my readers are educated, successful people, I look to you for proof of this. I ask you: Did your parents hold you responsible and accountable for your homework? You bet they did. And our kids need us to do the same for them.

Reason #4

Through doing homework, a child learns how to gain knowledge. By independently doing their homework, they start to establish the belief that "I have what it takes to learn." This is a powerful belief that can lead a person to great achievements in life. It gives a person a sense of competence with which to succeed.

If you have this sense about yourself that "you have what it takes to learn," let me ask you a few questions. How did you get this belief? Can you relate it to school and homework? How has it helped you in life? I rest my case.

Reason #5

Who was it who said, "More in life is accomplished through persistence than anything else?" Whoever it was succinctly put into words what all successful people eventually find out: Persistence pays off.

Parents can deliver this lesson through homework. Children needing to learn the value of persistence will provide you with ample opportunities for you to encourage them to persist. Sometimes they will even need you to insist that they persist.

As I talk to successful people, so often they give credit to their parents for their "you can do it" messages and encouragement to stick with it in spite of the struggle. Keep in mind, homework is supposed to be hard. Kids are meant to struggle over it. Struggle is a good thing, not a bad thing that children need to be spared from. Persistence can be taught through struggles over homework.

Reason #6

Time management can be learned through the process of doing homework. Many of today's young people could benefit from learning how to budget their time. I know this from the surveys I take from my audiences across the country. Parents consistently report their children either not doing their homework until the last minute or not getting it done at all.

In the following pages I'll discuss how you can use Smart Discipline to get your children motivated to do their homework on their own and in a timely fashion. Along the way, you may even be able to teach your kids the valuable lesson of how to postpone pleasure. Or, as earlier generations of parents put it, "Work comes before play."

THREE RULES CHILDREN NEED PARENTS TO INSIST UPON

Let me first acknowledge that some kids do not need these rules. These are those delightful kids who love schoolwork, breeze right through it, and are likely to work ahead in their textbooks. All these children need is your support and encouragement. For the rest, the three rules in this chapter will go a long way toward

- preventing and eliminating homework hassles.
- motivating "best of ability" quality.
- motivating "timely" completion.
- motivating independent work.

The following rules cover most of what you need to do as a parent in relation to homework. By insisting that these rules be followed, parents can help ensure that their children get the most out of the homework experience: high self-esteem, good grades, a sense of responsibility and accountability, self-confidence, persistence, and time management skills.

I mention the benefits again because the rules, though simple in theory, take time, patience, and diligence to implement. Consider them *your* homework. When you think about it, this makes sense. Parents can't expect their children to accrue all of these great benefits without themselves putting in a good measure of effort. As our parents have told us time and again, "There's no such thing as a free lunch!" So get ready. Here we go.

Rule #1

Establish a time for homework. As parents, we can either help our children set up a consistent time to do homework or leave it up to them to do it when they feel like it. Hmmm, let's see now. What choice should be made?

If you buy into the idea that homework is important and you want to communicate this to your children, there is only one choice: Establish "homework time." The very act of doing so communicates to your children that homework is a top priority in your house.

On average, an elementary school student may need up to half an hour a day, a middle school student an hour or so, and high school students up to an hour or two daily (more on some days for major papers, exams, and projects).

Based on the idea that our adult workday is typically eight hours and a child's school day is six hours, these amounts of time would seem reasonable. If your child's homework demands a great deal more or less time than this, it's time to sit down with your child's teachers and discuss why.

Many kids today have after-school activities, want to play when they get home, or face other circumstances that make doing homework after school difficult. However, there are some who both can and prefer to do it right after school. A good rule of thumb is to set "homework time" as early as possible, while allowing for a break after school. For some families, this may mean four P.M., while for others it may mean six or seven P.M.

To determine the time, I suggest having a family meeting. As adults do, children more willingly comply with decisions in which they participate. Three guidelines should be followed when making the decision:

1. Make it the same time each day if at all possible. This is the best way to establish a habit.
2. Make it so the completion time will be no later than seven P.M. for elementary school children, eight P.M. for middle schoolers, and nine P.M. for high schoolers. When you think about it, is homework likely to get done neatly and correctly after these times? Probably not. Besides, all of us, kids alike, need time for rest and relaxation.
3. All other activities such as phone calls and television should be postponed until homework time is over.

You can expect that after establishing homework time, a few problems will emerge. These will include such things as

- dragging out the task—and the agony (don't ask me why they do this; for some unknown reason, they just do)
- procrastination
- deal making
- assertions of "I don't have any homework"
- lost assignments
- books left at school
- miscellaneous creative excuses

We will deal with these and other "challenges" in the next chapter, where we present the fifteen top homework problems that plague parents—and their solutions. Suffice it to say here that establishing homework time will be easier determined than carried out. It will take time, patience, and persistence on your part. But it will be worth it. Problems will be prevented and successful life skills taught because of your efforts.

Rule #2

Establish a homework place. As our mothers taught us, "There is a time and a place for everything." And the place for homework is not at the kitchen table, on the phone, or in front of the television. Common sense dictates that these places are not conducive to learning. Nor do they give homework a place of importance. The "homework place" should be one of privacy, a place where your child goes during home-work time.

Ideally, it will be a place where your child can work privately with-out distraction from other people. It will also be stocked with whatever items he needs to complete his homework. For the most part, this means writing paper, pencils, pens, a pencil sharpener, and a computer if pos-sible. Special projects, of course, demand other items. These can be supplied on an "as needed" basis.

The whole idea of establishing a homework place is to help your child identify homework as a major responsibility. Therefore, it has a special time and place to be accomplished. In the same family meeting in which you establish the time, you can discuss the place.

Once you and your children have agreed upon their homework time and place, you are ready to discuss the third rule.

Rule #3
Homework is to be done alone. To explain this rule, review the fol-lowing points with your child:

1. Homework is a child's responsibility.
2. You, the parent, will answer questions when you can, but the child must complete the work.
3. You will occasionally check homework to see if it is done cor-rectly and neatly.

This is very similar to the way parents of baby boomers approached homework. That's interesting, because many baby boomers tend to do the opposite with their own kids, playing too strong a role in the completion of homework. Parents who do this run the risk of robbing their child of the homework benefits mentioned earlier—high self-esteem, good grades, responsibility, self-confidence, persistence, and time management skills. No parent wants to do this, but that's exactly what happens when a parent shoulders the responsibility for homework and studying.

While not intending it, this parent is giving her child the message "You don't have what it takes to be successful in school without my help." Sometimes parents with good intentions get trapped into doing this when they want to make sure their child does well in school. Their way of making sure is by hovering over them and supervising their studies. This, I admit, is tempting sometimes, especially when a child is struggling. But it is at just such a time that our children need us to insist that they do their homework on their own.

When you insist on rule number three, you will be giving your children the message that they have what it takes to be successful in school. Some children, especially those addicted to "parental help," will resist this message. They will argue in every way they can that they need their parents' help. This is understandable. They are afraid. But what they really need is a parent willing to say, "Yes, I understand it is hard, but homework is your responsibility and you can do it if you stick with it."

Lucky is the child who has a parent willing to give this message. I can hear some of you saying, "But you don't understand. My child really does need my help in order to pass." This is a very real issue for some, but please know that regardless of these fears, both you and your child will be much better off if you

- establish the rules.
- expect some dissent.
- remember the benefits.
- insist that the rules be followed.

Fifteen Common Homework
Problems (and Uncommon Solutions)

Let's dive right into the problems. Homework problems left unresolved can destroy a family's peace and a child's chance for success in school.

Too many times I've heard from families who spend their evenings anguishing and arguing over homework. Often the kids in these families decide they don't have what it takes to be successful in school. When this happens, it frees up 100 percent of their time to disrupt their families and their schools. Twenty-five percent of the kids in America make this decision and drop out of school. It's tragic. And it's time to take action! So let's take a look at some of the common problems and some uncommon but highly effective solutions.

PROBLEM #1
"I DON'T HAVE ANY HOMEWORK"

Sometimes it's true. Other times trusting parents are shocked to find out it was a lie. They usually find out too late: after they look into poor report cards and find out that homework wasn't handed in on time or at all.

How is a parent to know? "Trust, but verify" is my answer. Here is an example of what I mean:

Mom: Do you have any homework tonight?
Son (twelve years old): Nope.
Mom: I've been hearing that a lot lately. How come?
Son: I do it at school. The teachers give us time.

Mom: That's great, son. For the next few weeks, I want you to bring it home so I can look at it.

Son: Aw, Mom, that's stupid!

Mom: Negative comments aren't necessary. What is necessary is for you to show me your work.

Son: Oh, all right, if I have to.

The idea is this. Every child is assigned some schoolwork almost every day. As I mentioned earlier, some kids love it and do it willingly. Others avoid it out of frustration, disinterest, or dislike. Those children who avoid homework need parents willing to check up on their assignments.

Besides looking at school papers, check periodically with the teacher(s) and ask two questions: "Is my child handing in his homework on time?" "Is it done neatly and correctly?"

Once you start checking up on homework, you won't hear "I don't have any homework" nearly so often. That brings up the question, though, of what to do with "homework time" when there is no homework.

Some family psychologists and educators suggest that the time be filled with some form of schoolwork anyway. I would say it depends on the circumstances. If the child's grades are good and homework has been up to snuff, why worry about it? Let your child enjoy her night off. We all need them. If, however, homework and grades have been suffering, the homework time should be filled with schoolwork that can strengthen apparent weaknesses. To identify weaknesses and practice work that will help, confer with your child's teacher. If you show an interest, so will he. And he'll probably have some other great suggestions, too.

PROBLEM #2
"IT'S TOO HARD!"

If your child is complaining that her homework is too hard, one of several things may be occurring. Most often a parent interprets the "It's too hard" complaint to mean "I don't know how to do my homework." So the first solution is to review the instructions with your child to be sure she understands them. After doing so, be sure to send her back to do the work on her own.

Another possibility behind "too hard" is that she is seeking some attention and sympathy. This isn't unusual, either. All of us like some loving attention when we are doing something difficult. The thing *not* to do here is to try to convince her that it's not hard. This will only cause her to *prove to you* that it's too hard by not being able to do it. A better tactic is to respond with something like the following:

Daughter: "This math is too hard for me! I hate it!"
Mother: "Yes, algebra can be tough to understand, can't it?"
Daughter: "Yeah, especially factoring equations."
Mother: "I can remember having trouble with that, too."
Daughter: "Well, I guess I better go get started on it."

By letting your child know it's okay to feel the way she is feeling, you allow her to 1) feel good about herself; 2) feel good about you; and 3) let go of her negative feelings.

"Too hard" can also mean that the work is beyond your child's present level of comprehension and ability. Indicators that this might be the case include

- a consistent inability to do assignments correctly.
- failing grades on homework and tests.
- a consistent expression of frustration from your child over the subject matter.

If this is the case, the problem most likely will not resolve itself. However, the temptation that many parents face at this point, which should be resisted, is to help the child with the homework. It's okay to help some. But it is not helpful to sit with the child night after night and help him do his assignments. The teacher needs to know if your child can't do the work. You need to know, too. The sooner the better for your child.

When you find indicators that the work is beyond your child's current capabilities, it is time to meet with the teacher and ask for her help. Fortunately, most teachers are more than happy to assist a parent seeking help.

When you meet with the teacher, set your sights on

1. identifying the problem.
2. agreeing on a plan of action.
3. setting up ways and times to determine progress (or lack thereof).

After establishing these with the teacher, follow-through on steps one and two above are very important. Also important is changing whatever isn't working and trying different solutions such as tutoring.

In seeking alternative solutions, don't forget to ask your child what he thinks would help. I know of one mother who tried this with her seven-year-old son, who couldn't read. Every conventional method had been tried and failed. When asked what he thought might help, he suggested comic books. Mom and Dad said okay and let him pick some out. Several months later he was not only reading, but it was one of his favorite things to do.

PROBLEM #3
"I'LL DO IT LATER"

I wonder how many kids in America put off their homework until the last possible minute. According to my informal surveys of parents at my Smart Discipline seminars, it's a lot.

"I'll do it later" causes a couple of major problems. First of all, families end up fighting and bickering about it all night. Second, when it is done "later," it often gets done quickly and sloppily.

As noted in the previous chapter, the solution lies in rule number one: insistence on homework time. If procrastination is a problem, this rule needs to be enforced as consistently as possible. Also, it's a big help to suspend other privileges once homework time starts. You will want to let your children know what these are. Your list might include

- telephone calls
- television

- friends coming over
- video games
- going outside

Suspending all privileges until homework is done can work like a charm, but be careful. Often, children will plead to use the phone because they need to get either the assignment or some help from a friend. To counteract this, let your kids know all phone calls will have to be made and completed before homework time starts.

Some children, in order to watch a favorite TV show or get on the phone, will scurry through homework. The results are often less than satisfactory. If this becomes a problem with your kids, let them know that privileges don't start until homework is completed and checked for neatness and accuracy.

PROBLEM #4
"WILL YOU HELP ME?"

When parents are faced with requests from their children for help, their natural response is to provide that help. Giving assistance to our children is part of our job as parents. It not only helps them, but it makes us feel useful to boot.

In relation to homework, some help is fine. But it should be limited to helping a child to understand instructions and possibly helping with a couple of sample problems. The child should then be sent back to her "homework place" to complete the work. Doing so gives the message "You are competent to do your schoolwork."

To give more help than this can lead to problems. Some kids get addicted to help. This is understandable, as human nature typically causes us to seek the quick and easy way out when faced with the discomfort of trying to figure something out for ourselves. A child addicted to homework help will argue convincingly that she cannot possibly do her homework without your help.

Each time parents give in, they reinforce the child's need for help. They also reinforce the child's belief that she "doesn't have what it takes to do her schoolwork on her own."

So here's the catch-22. As a parent, you may well want to help your children with their homework when they ask, but you don't want to get them addicted to being helped or, worse yet, give your children the message that they are not capable of doing it on their own.

The solution to this dilemma lies in enforcing rule number three: Homework is to be done alone. The more a child resists complying with this rule, the more he needs you to insist upon it. Because of your insistence, he will eventually learn that he is competent to learn on his own. How wonderful! "You don't understand," some parents tell me. "If I don't help my child, he'll flunk."

My response is this: If your child can't do the work on his own, he should flunk. Big red Fs in the education process are not necessarily bad. They signify that something is the matter, and something should be done about it. Helping a child pass can circumvent this process.

Let's say that your eight-year-old son has a reading problem. So you work with him every night in his workbook, making sure all of his homework is done correctly. You do such a good job that the teachers don't catch the problem and your son makes it all the way to fourth grade. Now your son has a major problem, because he is in the fourth grade with second-grade reading skills. To avoid this problem, help a little and then insist he do the rest on his own. If he can't, make an appointment to meet with the teacher, as discussed in problem number two: "It's too hard!"

PROBLEM #5
"IT'S STILL NOT PERFECT"

So many tears get shed by kids because they can't do something "just right." For children who are perfectionists, it's all or nothing. Either it's perfect or it's worthless. How do parents respond? With the best intentions, we say things like "Oh, Jennifer, you shouldn't feel that way. Look at how nice your drawing looks. I love it." Or "You shouldn't be so hard on yourself, Clint. You got third place. That's not bad at all for someone who's only fifteen."

We say things like this hoping both to give our kids a healthier perspective on themselves and to spare them emotional pain. If your child is a perfectionist, it won't work. The more you reason one way, the more he'll reason the opposite. Denying a child's feelings almost always starts a tug-of-war, which the parent always loses.

Instead, to assist your perfectionist to achieve a healthier point of view, try either clarifying the feelings or identifying with your child. For example: "Jennifer, it seems like you are really disappointed in your drawing. Is that right?" Or, "I can remember a time when I lost a race, too. It was a regional cross-country race in which I could have qualified to go on to the state championships. But I lost. What a disappointment!" Such responses are much more likely to meet with positive responses than ones that contain the words *you shouldn't*. These words cause kids and adults alike to tune out and turn off.

In the extreme case of a child who is constantly whining that whatever it is isn't right, you may want to assert something like "It is okay to want things to be done right, and it is okay to feel bad that things aren't the way you want them. It is not, however, okay to whine or cry about it. If you want, we can talk about it and you can try to correct what you don't like. But no crying or whining allowed."

PROBLEM #6
"WHAT'S THE MATTER WITH IT? IT LOOKS OKAY TO ME!"

For every child in the world who is a perfectionist, I think there are ten who gloss over their mistakes without a thought. Although this attitude toward homework can be frustrating to parents, research indicates non-perfectionists get more accomplished than perfectionists. Unfortunately for these kids, grades are based on quality, not quantity.

Homework needs to be done correctly and neatly in order to help a child to develop the values mentioned earlier: high self-esteem, self-confidence, good grades, persistence, responsibility, and time management skills.

If this is a problem for your child, try this:

Step 1: Check homework on a daily basis. Also check schoolwork done at school.

Step 2: If the work is done sloppily, show your child what needs to be corrected. (You may want to point out examples of his work done correctly.)

Step 3: Send him back to redo the work. Do not allow privileges until it is done correctly.

If your children learn that you won't accept homework done poorly, they will start to do it right the first time.

One caution, though, is not to get too picky. Doing so can destroy a child's innate love of learning. If you have questions about homework quality, check with the teacher. She can tell you what her expectations are.

PROBLEM #7
"I'M NO GOOD AT . . ."

When a child says "I'm no good at" something, he most likely means one of the following three things:

1. He wishes he were good at it but needs help.
2. He believes he can't do it.
3. He has no interest in it whatsoever.

With so many possibilities, the easiest way to find out is to ask. For example:

Mandy (ten years old): I'm no good at math.
Dad: Sounds like you're having trouble in math. Is that right?
Mandy: Yeah. I'm just no good at it.
Dad: I'm wondering what makes you say you are no good at math.
Mandy: I don't understand any of my math homework, that's why.
Dad: So what do you think would help?
Mandy: I suppose I could call Cindy. She's good at helping me.

Clarifying feelings and asking for the child's solution works a lot better than succumbing to the temptation to do this:

Mandy: I'm no good at math.

Dad: Sure you are, honey.

Mandy: No, I'm not.

Dad: All you need to do is study harder and you'll do fine.

Mandy: No, I won't.

Dad: Well, you'd better. Without math you won't be able to go to college or get a decent job. You'd better get in there and buckle down.

Mandy: Well, I can't. College isn't important anyway!

You can see where this is headed. Both Mandy and her dad are likely to be so angry at one another that the evening will be ruined for both. Lucky is the child whose parent chooses to

1. clarify feelings; and
2. brainstorm solutions.

PROBLEM #8
"I'VE GOT A MAJOR PROJECT DUE"

Consider the following. You come home from work. You are tired and want to have supper and relax a little bit, perhaps catch up on some reading. But it's not to be. When you walk in the door your son tells you his science project is due tomorrow. He tells you it counts for 25 percent of his grade and asks if you have any suggestions for it. Like many parents, you get exasperated, give your child a lecture, and spend the rest of the night helping him throw together a science project. This is foolish. It doesn't teach anything about responsibility or time management.

If this is an all-too-familiar situation at your house, here is a different plan of action. It works well and prevents lots of problems.

Step 1: Have a family meeting to discuss major school projects.

Step 2: Tell your kids that from now on, if assistance or materials will be needed for a project, you are to be informed of the project when it is assigned. Tell them this will be the *only* time you will be willing to work out the details with them.

Step 3: Work out the details on projects of which you are informed in a timely fashion. Refuse to assist with projects "forgotten till the last minute."

Your kids may test you to see if you mean business. The only way to pass this test is by sticking to what you said. This, of course, is tough when you have a child wailing, "You don't love me!" and, "I'm going to get an F and it will be all your fault!"

At just such times, your child needs you to insist on sticking to your guns. If you do, she will learn that you mean what you say. She will also learn to plan ahead for projects.

PROBLEM #9
"I LEFT IT AT SCHOOL"

Did you ever notice that leaving their homework at school is never a problem for good students? For some reason, these kids always remember to bring home what they need to do their homework. Rather, it is the students having trouble with schoolwork who do.

This is no big problem if it happens just occasionally. But for the repeat offender, a plan of action is needed. I suggest the following:

Step 1: Buy your child an assignment book.
Step 2: Require that your child fill it out each day. If needed, require that she have the teacher sign it.
Step 3: Let her know that if for any reason she forgets her assignment book or homework, all privileges will be suspended for that evening. Let her know what privileges will be withheld, for example: television, telephone, video games, going outside, and having friends over.

If you follow this plan, your child will "forget" one day and protest how "unfair" you are. Most likely she will also have a barrage of both excuses and great reasons why you should give her another chance. Your child, I believe, will be best served if you respond with, "Yes, you do deserve another chance. You will get it tomorrow. As for today, no privileges."

PROBLEM #10
"HOMEWORK IS STUPID"

Negative attitudes are tough to deal with. I think our kids know it. Some even have an uncanny ability to use them against us. Let me tell you what I mean. In the normal course of events, parents nag their kids. They do so to prod them. It would seem necessary, because there isn't a child alive who consistently does what he is asked the first time. Unfortunately, as parents verbally prod their children, they are likely to pepper these prods with angry and critical comments. In response, children often sling back negative comments that are sure to send their parents up the wall. It usually goes something like this:

Mom: Jason, it's time to do your homework.

Jason: I'll do it right after this program is over, okay?

Mom: That's what you said an hour ago. I want you to do it right now.

Jason: C'mon, Mom. Just ten more minutes, okay?

Mom: Oh, all right, but then turn off the television. Okay?

Jason: No problem.

Mom (thirty minutes later): Jason, why are you still watching TV? You never listen to me. What is your problem, anyway?

Jason: Homework is stupid, that's what.

Mom: What do you mean, homework is stupid?

Jason: It just is. And so is school. I'm going to drop out when I'm sixteen anyway!

Conversations like these end up in screaming matches in which all sorts of ugly, hurtful comments are made.

Trying to reverse the course of the conversation once tempers flare is difficult to do. Prevention is the best tactic, but prevention isn't all that easy, either—especially if parent and child have fallen into the muddy, slippery rut of responding to each other in the way I just described. Change takes some real effort.

To change, keep in mind this rule of communication: If you change the way you respond to someone, she has to change the way she responds to you. You can prove this for yourself. Analyze any communication pattern you have with a loved one. Identify what you usually say and the likely responses. Then decide how you can respond differently the next time the pattern presents itself. Your results will be revealing, I'm sure.

If you have a child who makes negative comments about homework and school, try the same thing. For example, the mother in my example might think: It seems that almost every night I get into an argument with Jason over homework. What happens is usually this. He starts watching television and doesn't get to his homework. Then I start reminding him. He puts me off until I start nagging him. He then says something negative and I get furious and yell at him.

After identifying this pattern, this mother could brainstorm some alternate ways of responding, such as the following:

1. Discussing the problem with Jason when they're both calm and asking his ideas for a solution.
2. Letting Jason know that from now on the television will be turned off at seven P.M. every night and not turned back on until his homework is done.
3. Deciding to talk slowly and quietly in response to inflammatory statements. (This causes anger in both parties to subside.)

Once alternatives are thought out, one can be selected for use. It takes some time and effort to go through this process. But it can help break up major negative communication patterns.

Have patience with yourself when you try this process. Communication patterns are deeply ingrained, but they can be changed with effort and persistence.

PROBLEM #11
"I'LL DO IT WHEN YOU GET HOME"

With the many households in which both mom and dad work, lots of children either go home to an empty house or to a sitter after school. By the time the parents get home it's late, with meal preparation and housekeeping chores waiting. It sure would be nice if homework was already done, wouldn't it? Unfortunately, children often stall doing homework until a parent is there to "make them."

If this is a problem at your house, try the following tactic. Give your kids a choice. Tell them they may either have their homework done before you get home or wait to do it after you get home. However, if they choose the latter option, tell them there will be no privileges that evening. No television, no phone, no video games, and no visits with friends until homework is done. Such choices are motivating and can easily be modified to fit your situation. If you won't be home until it's too late for homework, insist that completed assignments be laid out for you to see when you get home.

You can give even more motivation to your children to get their homework done by making their weekend privileges dependent on its timely completion. For instance, let's say your daughter goes to the movies every Friday night. In this case, you tell her that her homework must be done each evening or no Friday night movie. Try it. You will be surprised how much better this works than screaming and yelling.

PROBLEM #12
"HOMEWORK ALWAYS TAKES ME ALL NIGHT"

Do you have a child who drags out his homework all night? If so, something should be done for the sake of everyone's sanity. Pondering over homework all evening can drive a whole family to distraction.

One solution is to suspend all privileges until homework is done. This strategy works like magic for most. Others are unfazed by it and dawdle all night anyway.

In such a case, insist on a starting and stopping time for homework. When homework time is over, collect the books and papers and put them away. The consequence of any homework left undone is between the children and their teachers.

This is a great lesson in living. On the job, a person has to learn to get her work done on time. If not, she has to explain to her boss and face the consequences. The more times it happens, the more severe the consequences. In this case, the consequences are between your child and his teacher. You are there only to consult and motivate as needed—and to teach a little time management on the side!

PROBLEM #13
"THAT'S NOT THE WAY THE TEACHER SAID"

Isn't it funny. Children come to us for help with their homework. We attempt to help them, whereupon the children often complain, "That's not the way the teacher said to do it!" Frustrating, isn't it?

If your child is an occasional perpetrator, you can usually have him explain how the teacher wants it done and then send him to go do it. If he's a constant perpetrator, plan ahead. Next time help is sought, ask: "How did your teacher say to do it?" If the response is, "I don't know," ask, "How can you find out?"

Usually your child can find out how to do something from either a friend or the teacher. While parents can often give them the help they seek, it can be much more helpful to direct them elsewhere. It teaches self-reliance. And it prevents complaints about the quality of your help!

PROBLEM #14
"WHY CAN'T I DO IT IN FRONT OF THE TELEVISION?"

Hmmm. Let me count the reasons:

1. It is virtually impossible to concentrate with the television on, so homework suffers.
2. Doing homework in front of the television sends the message that homework is not very important.
3. Doing homework in front of the television drags out the task.

Having reasons "why" you decided on something rarely appeases kids, though, and often just causes further arguing. Sometimes saying "Because I said so" is the best response. It cuts off the argument and allows both you and the child to go on to more important things.

It is important to note, though, that while television distracts from homework, music helps. Music facilitates memory and concentration. It works so well, in fact, that we can remember the words to songs we learned thirty years ago. Sometimes just hearing a song will bring back memories otherwise forgotten. So next time you insist that television must be off during homework time, allow music as long as it is played softly (loud music serves only to boost adrenaline, which is not conducive to sitting still and studying).

PROBLEM #15
"MY TEACHER'S UNFAIR"

Children complain about teachers. They say things like "My teacher gave me too much homework"; "My teacher is always picking on me"; and "The teacher didn't explain this so I could understand it." When faced with complaints about teachers, parents can choose from several responses.

The first two are both common and counterproductive. One choice is to ask for details about the complaint and then respond with something like "You're right. I'll talk to the teacher and get her straightened out!" Major harm is done to a child when such comments are made either to a child or within a child's hearing range. Kids who hear comments that put down teachers, no matter how well-intentioned, learn contempt and disrespect for teachers. This turns kids off to learning. To avoid harming a child's attitude toward learning, it is essential that any and all negative comments about teachers be kept from the ears of children.

Another way parents respond to complaints about teachers is by lecturing the child: "If you wouldn't waste so much time at school, I bet you could get all your homework done in study hall. I know I used to. The problem is you're just too concerned about what your friends are doing instead of concentrating on what you should be doing!" Again, parents make comments like this with good intentions. They think that a little good advice coupled with insightful comments about a perceived character flaw will cause a child to change his attitude and behavior. Instead, the attitudes and behaviors worsen.

In the more constructive responses, the parent listens and clarifies feelings. For example:

Jeff (coming in from school): My teacher stinks!

Dad: Sounds like you had a hard day at school.

Jeff: Yeah, well, it wouldn't have been so hard if it wasn't for Mrs. Jensen. She's always on my case for no reason.

Dad: Tell me more.

Jeff: Well, this is just one minor example. She told me she was sick and tired of me being late for class and the next time she was going to make me stay after school. That was so unfair. I was only ten seconds late. And besides, she never says anything to the other kids when they're late.

Dad: Let me see if I understand. You feel like Mrs. Jensen treats you unfairly and you are angry about it. Is that right?

Jeff: Yeah, and some days she really bugs me. Oh well, I guess I can handle her for now. School is out in three weeks, anyway.

In this example, Dad may well have had a strong urge either to come to his son's aid by putting down the teacher or to lecture his son and give him some advice. But Jeff was much better served when his Dad chose to listen and to clarify his feelings. By doing so, he gave his son three messages:

1. I care enough about you to take the time to listen to you.
2. It is okay to feel the way you feel.
3. You are competent enough to handle your own problems.

These are powerful and wonderful messages to communicate to a child. They make it well worth the time and effort it takes to listen and to clarify feelings.

PART FOUR

Parenting Mistakes to Avoid and Common Parenting Concerns

Seven Key

Mistakes Parents Make

As a family therapist, I have encountered numerous heartbroken parents who feared they had failed their children. One such parent approached my wife and me as we sat in a doughnut shop early one morning. He was a new acquaintance of ours who had attended one of my Smart Discipline workshops the night before.

With a smile, Jerry (not his real name) greeted us. But the smile turned to a grimace as he related the following: "Larry, I learned last night at your lecture why my twenty-eight-year-old son won't talk to me anymore. And I learned why he hasn't been able to keep a job even as a short-order cook."

Jerry stated, his voice getting more and more strained, "It's all my fault—the mistakes you talked about last night were the ones I made with my son. I made them over and over again. I can see it so clearly now. It's no wonder he doesn't want to come around anymore and why he has such a miserable life. My constant criticisms, though well-intentioned, destroyed both his self-confidence and our relationship!"

I felt pretty inadequate in my attempt to console Jerry in the middle of the crowded doughnut shop. "Jerry, I can see your pain and I can feel your pain. I'm sure you're like all of us parents, though. Everything we do with our kids we do with the best of intentions. None of us gets up in the morning thinking, I wonder what I can do today to screw up my kid. Isn't that right?"

"Yes," Jerry said. "I wanted nothing but the best for my son, but I failed him in all the ways you talked about. I guess what they say is true . . . the road to hell is paved with good intentions."

The pain on Jerry's face and in his voice is difficult to describe. As positively as I could, I said to him, "Jerry, let me give you some good news. You can always begin again with your son. It is never too late. As time goes on, opportunities will come up for you to turn things around between the two of you. With the new knowledge and insights you gained last night, you are in a better position than ever to heal your relationship and help your son improve his life."

"Are you sure it's not too late?" Jerry asked.

"No, it's never too late with kids," I replied. "It only becomes too late if we give up on them. As long as you hang in there and keep trying, there is always hope."

How things turned out for Jerry and his son I don't know. But I do believe that there is always hope if we are willing to keep on trying to be a positive influence in our children's lives.

I also believe that there a number of major mistakes we can avoid as parents so we don't have to face the heartbreak Jerry experienced. Knowing what these mistakes are is half the battle. The other half is to be forearmed with a positive plan for what to do instead.

Knowing what you are going to do in advance of difficult parenting situations gives both you and your children a wonderful advantage. It allows a lot more win-win situations for everyone involved.

Keep in mind that you can't change everything at once. To try would be to fail. It is far better to implement one change at a time.

Remember, too, that despite our best intentions, change is tough. When we make changes we are prone to procrastination, to making mistakes and backsliding. All are normal. And most of us, including our kids and spouses, fight change, no matter how positive. Change is scary, and we human beings resist it.

The good news is that we all have the capacity, if we persist in our efforts, to raise successful kids. To all of you who would strive to do so, we say, "Bravo, keep up the good fight! And never, never, never give up on your children, no matter what!"

MISTAKE #1
NOT LEARNING FROM YOUR MISTAKES

Many times I have started my parenting lectures with the following story. It is my favorite parenting story.

Every year Bill and Bob would go hunting together. This year they decided to go into the mountains of Montana to go elk hunting.

Both Bill and Bob wanted to return to their favorite hunting lodge. It sat on a beautiful secluded lake accessible only by seaplane. So they hired a plane and a pilot to fly them there.

As the pilot glided the plane over to the dock, Bill and Bob asked him to return to pick them up in a week. The pilot agreed, and Bill and Bob disembarked.

They had a lot of luck and shot six elk. Luckily, they were able to get the elk down to the dock just in time for the pilot's return. As the pilot tied the seaplane to the dock, Bill and Bob started to tie the elk to the pontoons of the plane. That was the way you got the elk out of the mountains.

But the pilot counted those elk and said, "Hey, wait a minute! You can't put six elk on this plane. It will never get us out of the mountains. This plane will hold only four elk."

Bill and Bob started to argue with him. "Oh come on!" Bob said. "Last year we had six elk and a plane just like yours. Same-size engine, same-size wingspan. The wind conditions were even the same—and we had six elk!"

After a bit of haggling, the pilot finally agreed and helped them tie all six elk to the pontoons of the plane. Then they all got in the plane and took off.

About fifteen minutes into the flight, they crashed into the side of the mountain. After thirty minutes or so, Bill and Bob came to and climbed out of the wreckage.

Bill took a look around, turned to Bob, and said, "Bob, where in the dickens do you suppose we are?"

Bob took a look around and said to Bill, "It looks like we're about two miles from where we crashed last year!"

I call that a parenting analogy, because isn't that the way we often are as parents? Our child does something we told him not to do. So we spank, yell, lecture, threaten, or carry on as we always do when our child disobeys.

What happens? Two hours later, he is right back doing the same thing. And so what do we do? Probably the same thing that didn't work two hours ago!

Someone once said that the definition of insanity is doing the same thing over and over again and expecting different results. Maybe this explains why our kids so often look at us as if we are crazy.

Joking aside, we parents tend to repeat our mistakes again and again. This, of course, is not by intention. Rather, we do so because we are human and fall victim to our habit patterns, despite our best intentions.

We also repeat our behavior because it worked for us in the past at some point and we reason that it should work again if we keep doing it. This reasoning reminds me of the difference between humans and rats (bear with me, this is a joke with a point). You can teach both rats and humans to run mazes. The difference between rats and humans is that if you remove the cheese from the maze, the rats will stop running the maze and humans won't!

Sometimes, even though we know what we're doing isn't working, we don't know of a better choice. So we do what we know even though it doesn't work very well.

This is to be expected, especially in light of how busy parents are today. There is little time to stop and learn better ways of parenting. This leaves most parents responding to difficulties with their children as they come up. So, in effect, parenting choices are guided more by emotional reactions than by informed forethought.

If we hope to act "sanely" as parents, then thinking things out in advance is a must. Here are a few suggestions that can help.

1. Read a parenting book every couple of months. Libraries and bookstores offer a broad selection. If you are looking for a book on a particular topic, ask a reference librarian. These people can find anything, *and* they love to help.

2. Attend a parenting workshop. Consult your friendly librarian, local hospital, school, mental health center, church, parenting center, or United Way agency. You will be surprised by what a wide variety is available and at little or no cost.

3. Join a support group. Two that seem to be gaining popularity are Tough Love and a group for parents of children with ADHD called CHAD. Other support groups are available for parents of children with physical problems and can be accessed through your local hospitals. To get information, call the hospitals in your area and ask for the community relations department (these are also great people who love to help).

4. Consult a family therapist. Sometimes problems require professional help. What often stops parents from seeking the help they need is either financial constraints or an attitude something like "In our family, we solve our own problems." Most communities now have agencies and church-based counseling centers that provide counseling at little cost. Many private therapists will also agree to sessions at a reduced fee if you ask. But you need to ask. As to the "we'll fix it ourselves" attitude, I respond with, "Yes, it is good to solve one's own problems. It is also completely understandable to want to keep family matters private. However, as parents we can't begin to know about everything or to be able to fix every problem that occurs with our children. As tough as reaching out for help can be, sometimes we need to do it for the sake or our children." If you do decide to get outside help, do not make the mistake of deciding family therapy won't work because the therapist you consulted wasn't able to help resolve your problems. If this happens, don't blame the process. Find another therapist who can help, just as you would if you had a physical ailment and the doctor you first went to was unsuccessful at helping you.

MISTAKE #2
SAYING NO AND THEN CHANGING YOUR MIND

Every parent has either experienced or witnessed the following scene. You are waiting in the checkout line in the grocery store. A mother (or father—it makes no difference) has a three-year-old in her grocery cart. The child points at some candy and says, "Can I have a candy bar?"

The parent quickly responds, "No, honey, that would rot your teeth and you wouldn't want to go to kindergarten with false teeth, now, would you?"

The child insists, "But I neeeed it. I'm hungry!"

The mom tries to reason with him: "No, you don't need it. You may want it, but you don't need it. Besides, we are going to have supper when we get home." The mom then turns to start unloading her cart onto the counter.

Taking advantage of his parent's turned back, the little boy snatches the candy bar in question. Mom turns around just in time to see him and commands, "Now, Timothy Allen Blakely, you put that right back!"

"No!" yells Timothy Allen as he squishes the candy bar in his fist.

Mom says, "Give me that candy bar right now!"

"No!" Timothy says, holding the candy bar out of Mom's reach.

In desperation, Mom slaps him on the other hand. Timothy relinquishes the candy and starts to cry. As everyone in line turns to look, he turns up the volume, kicks his feet wildly, and screams, "I want it, Mommy, *I want it!*"

So what does Mom do? We all know the answer, because most of us have done it. Mom says, "Oh, all right, rot your teeth out, but don't come to me when all the other kids laugh at your false teeth!"

Why do we do that kind of thing? We do it mainly because we need a quick fix to the situation: when we give in, the child stops screaming and the people stop staring. It's as simple as that.

The trouble is, if we do this kind of thing too often, we quickly teach our child a lesson: If his parent says no, he needs to make his parent as miserable as possible until she says yes. In short, children master blackmail at an early age and refine it to a science by the time they become teenagers.

To spare both your children and yourself from battling all the time, try one of the following when faced with a request you are not too fond of:

1. Instead of responding with either "Yes" or "No" to a request from your child, respond with, "Let me think about it." This has two advantages. First, while you are thinking about it, chances are your child will be "good as gold." Second, it gives you some time to think about your answer and whether or not you are will-

ing to stick with it regardless of the contention it might cause if the answer is "No."

2. Give a choice. For example: "Would you rather have the candy bar or would you rather have cake tonight for dessert?" Or, to a teenager arguing about going out, you might say, "Would you rather go to the movies tonight, or would you rather be allowed to go to the dance tomorrow night?" Many kids respond well to choices. Often it allows for compromise and win-win situations.

3. Ask questions. For instance, the mom in the grocery store might ask a series of questions:
   a. "What kind of candy bar do you like best?"
   b. "Are you hungry?"
   c. "Do you like candy or gum better?"
   d. "If we got the candy, when would you want to eat it?"
   e. "Would you be willing to have gum instead?"

   Just by the very act of asking questions, you will be giving the message to your children that you are listening to their requests and that you care about their desires. This alone will make them more reasonable.

4. Give them their request in fantasy. One of the most loving and memorable things my mother ever did for me was to give me a Jaguar XKE in fantasy when I was sixteen. I was telling her how much I wanted one, and she said, "I wish I could give you one right now. You deserve to have a beautiful car like that!" Not only did she give me the car in fantasy, but she did something few parents do: she did not negate the experience with a "but." In other words, she did not say, "I wish I could give you one. But you know, Larry, those cars are way out of our price range and we could never afford something like that."

   In our grocery store example, Mom might have used this last strategy to avoid the struggle by saying, "Timothy, I wish I could let you have a candy bar right now. You are a really good boy!" Can't you just see Timothy smiling, along with all the people in line?

All of these responses take some forethought, but the effort is well worth it. In fact, with a little practice you will become a master at teaching your children that you love them and want the best for them even when you say "No."

MISTAKE #3
LEAVING TEENAGERS ALONE WHEN YOU GO OUT OF TOWN

All parents are faced at some point with the decision of what to do with their teenagers when they need to go out of town. The decision was simple when their children were younger. You either got a baby-sitter or you took them with you. Now they're too big for baby-sitters and they don't want to go with you, so what do you do?

What most of us do is sit down with them and tell them we are going to trust them to stay alone and out of trouble while we are out of town. We give them strict instructions on what they can and cannot do while we are gone. And we make them swear, under penalty of being grounded for a year, that they will not have a party at the house while we're gone. They, of course, take an oath to obey the rules you have set forth.

What follows next is predictable and commonplace across generations (in other words, we did it, too). Either your child or her friends start to make plans for what to do in your absence. Too often this includes plans for a party, complete with booze garnered from your liquor supply and that of the friend's parents. This scenario happens daily in homes all across our country. And it is not only common to the present generation of teenagers, it was common in our generation as well.

Fortunately, the consequences are often negligible: we come home to not much more than a mess to clean up and a stern lecture to mete out.

But then there are the tragic outcomes that seem to happen more and more frequently. I am reminded of one I read about in which a school principal and his wife left town for the weekend and left their sixteen-year-old son to man the house.

On Saturday evening he had a party for over a hundred kids. One group left the party with a drunken teen at the wheel. They had an accident; one died and two were disabled.

Isn't it curious that we can look back on our own teenage years and see what mistakes our parents made (like trusting us to act right when they left town) and still repeat the same mistake with our own kids? When I was growing up, my friends and I lived for the weekends when someone's parents left town. I remember one weekend when my parents left me at home alone; one of my friends and I drank a fifth of my father's gin in less than half an hour.

I got so drunk, I blacked out. I also got so sick that I ran outside and lay in a snowbank to try to sober up. Ever since then I haven't been able to drink hard liquor—not by choice, but because my body seems to view it as poison and my throat will not let it pass. In retrospect, I'm sure that I had alcohol poisoning and I am lucky to have survived. Perhaps you can recall similar things that happened when you were a teen.

Now I know that not all teens are going to go off the deep end when their parents leave them alone overnight. But it's a good bet that they may well do something they shouldn't. It certainly leaves them open to a good deal of peer pressure to misbehave.

What I suggest is arranging for someone to check on your teens at both regular and unscheduled times when you are out of town. If your teens know someone will be checking on them, they will be a lot less likely to misbehave. It also gives them an acceptable excuse when confronted by peer pressure, since they can respond with, "I can't have a party at my house because my uncle [parents' friends, neighbors, and the like] keeps coming over to check on me."

One side note here. If your child loudly protests and accuses you of not trusting her, watch out. This may be a real indicator that she wants to be left alone for a reason. And it probably isn't a good one. I think a good response is, "I trust you, and it's my job as a parent to check up on you at all times to make sure that you're okay."

MISTAKE #4
NOT LISTENING EFFECTIVELY

Children and adults alike have a huge need to be listened to and understood. This is evidenced by the hundreds of millions of dollars we spend each year in the United States on therapists, counselors, social workers, psychologists, and psychiatrists. Mainly these professionals are trained to do one thing: listen effectively.

When someone listens to us effectively, we feel accepted and understood. We relax and we feel good. It even makes us feel worthwhile as a person to have someone take time to sit down and focus on what we are saying. Perhaps best of all, having someone listen to us helps us straighten out our emotions and our thinking.

Given all of these benefits, it is no wonder that we spend millions each year to be listened to. What is too bad is that we have to pay some-one to do it. You would think that we could satisfy this need for one another, in our families. Actually, we can. But to do so, we have to change the way we respond when our kids talk to us.

First, to listen effectively a few bad habits have to be overcome. When kids talk, parents tend to jump in automatically with some great advice about what their child should do. The problem with giving advice is that it tends to be a real turnoff to the person who is talking. The last time you told someone about one of your problems, were you looking for advice or did you just want someone to listen to you and understand your side of the story? Most likely it was the latter.

Another parental tendency is trying to talk children out of their feelings. Let's say five-year-old Jason comes out of his bedroom crying and sobs, "There are monsters under my bed!" The typical parent response is, "No, there aren't. Let me show you." The parent then goes about showing Jason why he shouldn't be afraid.

It sounds like a reasonable response, but the trouble is in its inher-ent message that the child should not feel the way he is feeling. If this happened only once in a while, it wouldn't be so bad, but it happens constantly in communication between parents and children. Parents want their children to feel better as quickly as possible, and because they can easily see the error in their children's thinking, they point out why they should not feel as they do. The basic message is, "You shouldn't feel that way, and let me tell you why."

The reason why this doesn't work very well is twofold. First, when you tell someone not to feel the way he is feeling, it causes him to hold even tighter to the way he is feeling. And while you are trying to tell him why he shouldn't feel that way, he is trying desperately to justify the way he feels. It's an automatic human response.

Unfortunately, too, when a child is essentially told not to feel the way he is feeling, he tends to feel misunderstood and rejected by his parents. If that pattern of communication is repeated over the years, the child finally gives up and stops communication with his parents at any meaningful level. If instead you clarify your child's feelings and tell him it's natural to feel that way sometimes, he will feel accepted and understood. And he will be able to let go of the feeling.

The third common mistake in listening effectively is paying only half attention when the child is talking. The common scenario is a child coming to talk about something and the parent continuing to do whatever she is doing. The child notices the inattention and says, "Mom, are you listening to me?" The mother says, "Yes, honey, go ahead. I'm listening." But she's really only half listening, and the child knows it. Unwittingly, the parent is giving her child the message that he isn't important enough for Mom to stop and listen to him.

To demonstrate the power of this nonverbal message in my workshops, I ask the participants to pair off and decide which of them will be A and which B. Then I ask the B group to step outside the room for a few minutes to think about a particular topic so they can come back and express their ideas to their partners when they return.

While they are out of the room, I instruct the A group to be great listeners when their partners return. I tell them that to be a great listener is to

- make and maintain eye contact.
- ask open-ended questions.
- clarify feelings.

I also ask them to refrain from giving advice and from trying to change their partner's thinking or feelings.

Then I tell them that when I give a prearranged signal, I want them to turn into "bad" listeners. In other words, I want them to break eye contact and to stop asking questions and clarifying feelings.

The results of this exercise are dramatic. When the B group returns and starts talking, the room comes alive with energy. It's almost electrifying. Then, when I give the signal for the As to become "bad" listeners, the response is just as dramatic. The room becomes silent. The energy dissipates. A "dead" feeling pervades the room.

After a minute or so, I put a halt to the exercise, much to my own and everyone's relief. Then I ask group B to describe their experience. I will never forget one of the first responses I received, in Bismarck, North Dakota. One woman related her experience with, "My partner was my husband. When I first came into the room and sat down, it was wonderful. My husband turned his chair toward me and he gave his full attention to what I was saying. He asked me questions and seemed genuinely interested in my thoughts and feelings on the issue. It was really great. But then all of a sudden he changed and went back to the way he is at home!"

You can try this exercise with your family members and experience the same dramatic results. Here are the dos and don'ts.

Do

1. Establish eye contact.
2. Stop doing what you are doing.
3. Ask nonjudgmental and open-ended questions.
4. Clarify feelings.

Don't

1. Give advice.
2. Try to change feelings.

These guidelines seem simple, although they take a lot of patience and practice to do effectively. But the payoff is incredible. The reward for your efforts will be a strong, loving relationship with your child, and a child who will come to you for advice when he needs it!

MISTAKE #5
NOT INSISTING ON INVOLVEMENT IN
SCHOOL, COMMUNITY, AND CHURCH ACTIVITIES

Some children insist on being involved in everything they possibly can. These children tend to grow up to be quite successful, and they are likely to keep themselves out of serious trouble.

The most important thing that a parent can do to ensure that children stay out of trouble is to support his children in extracurricular activities of all sorts. Kids who are "involved" are much more likely to shun trouble than the kids who are just "hanging out."

I heard a juvenile judge put it succinctly: "Rarely do I have a teenage offender in front of me who was brought up in church." Involvement in positive group activities keeps young people off the streets and out of trouble. It's a fact.

For those of you who are running all over town to get your children to all their activities, I say, "Bravo! Keep up the good work. All your efforts will pay off. As difficult as it is to keep up with all the running around, it is nothing compared to the heartbreak of standing in front of a judge with your child."

Some kids shun involvement like the plague. No matter what you try to get them involved in, they come up with every reason they can to avoid being involved in group activities. If you force them to go, they complain the whole time, drag their feet, and quit at the first opportunity.

Unfortunately, when children put up all this fuss, parents usually give up. When this happens everyone loses. The child loses all of the fun as well as the lessons she would have learned about how to function successfully in a group. The parent loses the positive peer pressure his child would experience to stay out of trouble.

To prevent these losses takes a parent willing to stand his ground and insist on involvement in at least several organizations or activities. In my opinion, it is one of the most important things we can do for our children's benefit.

If you have a child who is reluctant to participate, keep the following in mind:

1. Often children who are reluctant to participate in activities are simply afraid because they are shy or fear they won't be able to do as well as the other kids. If you think this might be the case with your child, even if he denies it, tell him it is natural to be afraid and that it is okay. Realize that the fear will dissipate after a few weeks (and most likely he will love it). You might even want to relate true stories from your childhood of times when you were afraid to join a group.

2. Let your child have a say in what activities and groups to join, but if she can't or won't decide, decide for her. Insist that church activities be part of the mix (if you don't already have a church, you may want to find one with a strong youth program to join).

3. If your child has given an activity a fair chance and wants to quit, insist that he choose something to replace it. Don't be surprised if, when your child learns it isn't an option to stay at home and do nothing, he decides to continue with the same activity.

4. Realize that children need to try out many different activities to find what they are good at and enjoy. Quitting something that a child doesn't enjoy is not necessarily bad as long as it is replaced by some other positive activity.

5. Decide what the consequences are going to be if your child refuses to participate. When our children became teens and needed some extra motivation to go to church, we provided it with a rule: "If you don't go to church, you lose all privileges for the rest of the day." One of our kids tested us to see if we were serious. She found out we were and, unfortunately for her, it was the day of her best friend's birthday party. The rest of our kids decided not to test the rule!

Every bit of effort that you put into motivating your children to participate in school, community, and church activities will be worth it, both for you and for your children. It will help keep your children out of trouble, and it will teach them how to work successfully with a group of their peers, as well as with people in authority.

MISTAKE #6
NOT CHECKING ON YOUR CHILDREN

How many times, when you were growing up, did you tell your parents that you were going one place when you knew you were going another? Or lie to your parents about what you were going to be doing while you were gone? The typical answer I get from participants in my seminars is, "Too many to count."

Isn't it surprising, then, that we blindly trust our children to tell the truth when they leave the house? I'm not saying that all kids lie about where they are going or what they are doing, but I know it happens a lot—from both personal and professional experience.

Many of us who deceived our parents when we were growing up might say, "Ah, so what? It wasn't that big a deal." And in truth, for a lot of us it wasn't. We didn't go off and do anything that bad. Today, though, we live in a different world. Kids can get themselves into a lot of trouble quickly if they end up in the wrong place at the wrong time.

Just recently I heard about a young man who was an Eagle Scout who was arrested for armed robbery. As it turned out, he was in a car with some other guys when one of them jumped out, ran into a convenience store, robbed it, and got back into the car. The Eagle Scout didn't even know it had happened. But he was guilty just the same, because he was in the "getaway car." Don't you know his parents were incredulous when they found out he'd been arrested? I can just imagine them saying something like "That's impossible. You must have the wrong person. Our son told us he was going to the library to study."

While I know it's a huge hassle, checking up on your children's whereabouts is essential in today's world. If your child knows you are likely to check up on him, he will have a good reason to "just say no" to negative peer pressure, saying something like "Nah, I can't do that 'cause my parents are always checking up on me!"

To help your child "just say no," here are a few suggestions:

1. When your child wants to spend the night at someone's house, always talk to the other parents beforehand about the plans for the evening (even if your child is a teenager). The more they protest and try to talk you out of it with complaints that you "don't trust them" and are "embarrassing them," the more you should stand your ground. You will most likely be pleasantly surprised that the other parents will welcome your call.

2. When your child is in middle school, junior high, and high school, stay involved with his teachers. Most parents are involved with the school and with their children's elementary school teachers but discontinue their involvement when their children get older. This usually happens because children

loudly protest that it's "embarrassing" and "nobody else's parents are doing it." Tell them you are sorry that they are embarrassed and you are especially sorry that other parents are shirking their parental duties, but that you have no intention of doing so! You are especially justified in doing this because the greatest single predictor of student success is parental involvement in school.

3. Let your children know that part of your job as a responsible parent is to check up on them. Tell them you love them and trust them, but that it is just part of your job as a parent to do so. Then give them a hug and a kiss, send them out the door, and tell them to have a good time. Then check up on them. At the point when you think you can trust them completely, check up on them anyway.

4. Be reasonable. Checking up on them doesn't mean being overprotective or watching their every move. It means making reasonably certain they are where they are supposed to be and doing what they are supposed to be doing.

MISTAKE #7
GETTING INTO POWER STRUGGLES

If you have a strong-willed child, you especially don't want to make this mistake. Power struggles between parents and strong-willed children typically end up in disaster for parent and child alike. For some children, it's no big deal when you ask them to do something and they say no; you just apply a little reasoning or pressure and they comply. Or if they feel strongly about something, you can reach a compromise.

This isn't the case with strong-willed children. From birth they take pride in not doing what their parents want them to do. They love to argue and always, always want the last word! If you have a strong-willed child, you know just what I mean. Ten times a day you seem to end up in a hassle over things that should be simple.

So, what's a parent to do? Here are a few suggestions that will prevent a lot of recurring hassles and, at the same time, increase the level of your child's cooperation.

1. Having a structured system of discipline can be a great help. One like Smart Discipline with rules and consequences is ideal. Having a system of discipline gives a strong-willed child the sense of control he needs. It will also help you deal with things more consistently and without losing your "cool."

2. Give choices as often as possible. Again, by doing so, you help fulfill your strong-willed child's need to feel in control. An example is, "Would you rather wear your blue sweater today or your red one?" or, "Do you want to do your homework now, or would you rather skip television tonight and do it after supper?"

3. Analyze the pattern of your power struggles. When you are calm and rational (which might not be too often if you live with a strong-willed child), sit and write down the sequence of events in a typical power struggle. It might look something like this:
   - I tell Anna to do something and she says, "I don't want to."
   - I tell her she has to.
   - Anna says, "You can't make me."
   - I tell her she'd better do as I ask or she will be in big trouble.
   - Anna says, "I don't care," goes in her room, and slams the door.
   - I say, "Oh, the heck with it, I'll just do it myself."

4. Once you have written out the sequence of a typical power struggle, brainstorm what you might do differently. Ask yourself questions like the following:
   - Is there some way I could frame my request as a choice?
   - Am I making a request or a command?
   - Is there a better time to ask her?
   - If I ask her, am I willing to compromise?
   - If I ask her, am I willing to follow through with a consequence if she refuses?
   - Could I ask in a different tone of voice?
   - What else could I change about the interaction?

5. Make a concerted effort to express appreciation when your child complies with your request. Like all children, strong-willed children do better and cooperate more often if they feel appreciated.

While strong-willed children can be quite frustrating to a parent, the upside is that they can become strong and valuable leaders. To help them put their strengths to good use, make sure you encourage them every day in any way you can. And insist on their being involved in school, community, and church activities. The more they are involved in positive group activities, the more practice they will get at cooperating with others.

The Most Frequent
Questions Parents Ask Me

This last chapter contains the questions that people ask me after the Smart Discipline seminars, in letters and in e-mails. You will likely find the situations described in the questions to be similar to ones that you face. If you have other questions, please feel free to e-mail them to me at larry@smartdiscipline.com. You may also want to sign up for the Smart Discipline Tip of the Day at smartdiscipline.com.

It is my hope that by reading this chapter (and book), you will find the information you need to help your children grow up to be both happy and successful in life. If this book helps you in any manner to do this, then my goal in writing it will have been accomplished!

Dear Larry,

Last week I took my son along with a friend to the mall to get a CD, at which time my son told me, "Get out of the store. You're embarrassing me with that big zit on your face. Go sit outside until we're done."

I was devastated. I didn't know what to do or say, so I went outside and waited. When they came out we went home. Since then there has been a rather stony silence between the two of us. It's terribly uncomfortable, but I don't know how to get past it. What do you think?

—A Mom with a Lot More than a Zit

Dear Mom,

I'm assuming your son is between twelve and fourteen, as this sounds like the insensitive statement of a child in that age range. And I am assuming that his father is not in the picture for you to go home and report the affront to (as most sons would know that their fathers would ground them for a month or two for saying such an awful thing).

Since your child, and I emphasize "child," is at the forefront of his teenage years, it is critical that you establish yourself as a loving, firm authority figure in his life. Every teenager desperately needs an authority figure to steer him or her toward the "good" in life and away from the "bad."

Sit down with your son immediately and ask him, "Are you aware that you hurt my feelings deeply at the mall the other day?" Regardless of how he responds, tell him exactly how his actions made you feel and ask him for an apology. If he cannot bring himself to apologize or if he shrugs it off, insist on getting some family counseling. Not as punishment, but because your son has little insight into the effects of his actions and even less empathy for other people. If this is left unchecked, it could lead to much greater acts of unkindness.

If, on the other hand, you are able to have a good talk with your son and he is genuinely remorseful for what he did, give him another chance. Tell him that while you were devastated by what he said you are willing to forgive him this time as long as he promises never to act that way again. You might also ask him at this point what he would deem an appropriate punishment should he ever relapse. Come to an agreement on what this punishment might be, give him a hug, and let go of it. Most likely it will not recur, but, if it does, consider the counseling route. The two of you very likely will need some help in remedying the situation.

Dear Larry,

I have a three-year-old son who clings to me constantly. He doesn't say much. He doesn't even whine much. But boy, does he ever cling. Wherever I go, there he is. I can barely go to the bathroom without him clinging to my leg.

I've heard of being a "mama's boy," but this is ridiculous. I love him dearly, but I've got to find some way of prying him off of my leg before I go absolutely nuts. Give me a plan and I will put it into action!

—*A Mom with Child Attached at the Knee*

Dear Attached Mom,

Here's the plan. Go to the store and buy half a dozen inexpensive toys. Keep them in the bag and show the bag of toys to your son. Let him pick a toy out of the bag to play with and set that toy out where he can see it. Tell him he can play with it later but that right now he needs to stay with you for the next half an hour.

Keep him right by you, even reminding him to keep hold of your leg. If he lets go, be nice about it, but say, "No, you can go play later. Right now I want you to stay by Mommy." After thirty minutes, let him go play with the toy.

Repeat this procedure the next day with a different toy from the bag. On the third day get out the bag again, but this time when he picks out a toy, give him a choice: "Would you rather play now in the living room, or do you want to stay with Mommy and play later?"

Keep repeating this last procedure until he finally says, "I want to go play." When he does, make a big deal of how "big" he is, how he can play on his own, and how he doesn't have to stay by Mommy all the time. When your husband comes home, make a big deal of telling him about it in front of your child.

Within a week your child should no longer be grafted to your leg.

Dear Larry,

My twelve-year-old son cries at the drop of a hat. If you just give him a look of disapproval, he cries. And if you tell him "No" or admonish him for something, he starts sobbing. This frustrates my husband and me terribly.

While we know it's the wrong thing to do, we normally throw up our hands and tell him to "forget it." But we really don't know how to handle the situation differently. Nothing we have tried works.

—*Mother of a Crybaby*

Dear Mom,

How frustrating it is to have a child constantly shed tears over minor events. However, some children are highly sensitive, far more so than other children. I know there is a lot of talk these days about raising children who are "emotionally intelligent," but this does not apply to highly sensitive children. They may be perfectly intelligent in every way, but they feel their feelings and emotions more strongly than other people do. There are many adults who are highly sensitive as well.

Knowing this may help a little to reduce your level of irritation and frustration. This is important, because if you act irritated and frustrated when your child cries, you will only worsen the crying.

It would be highly beneficial to both you and to your son if you can make a decision to "stay in your head" and out of your emotions when your son cries inappropriately. If you can, patiently sit down with him and help him put some words to how he is feeling. Say things like "It sounds like you are really disappointed right now, is that right?" or "Tell me what you are feeling right now. Are you angry or are you frustrated?"

Once you get him talking and identifying his feelings, the tears will start to dry. The more you are able to do this, the more he will start to replace his crying with his newfound ability to communicate his feelings verbally.

This process will take a while and a lot of patience, but it is a wonderful thing to do for a child. Your child will benefit by learning to express his emotions and will at the same time learn that he can come to you and talk about what he's feeling. This is something that few children grow up with. Those who do are very lucky indeed.

Dear Larry,

I'm about to have my fourth child and I hate the thought of all the jealousy from my other kids that my new baby will cause. For once it would be really nice if bringing a baby home would be greeted with joy instead of jealousy. Any suggestions?

—*A Very Pregnant Mother*

Dear Pregnant Mom:

Wow! Four kids. That's wonderful. And you're absolutely right. Bringing a baby home should be cause for great joy. Realistically, though, this blessed event also commonly gives rise to sibling jealousy. Fortunately there is a wonderful cure. Here it is.

At different times when you are feeding your new baby, have one (and only one) of your children come over to sit by you. When he or she does, talk to your baby and say something like "Jessica, I want you to meet your big sister Andrea. She is a really neat person. Andrea is very caring, kind, and smart, and she loves to laugh. Andrea is also really good at making friends and her favorite hobby is to read. You are very lucky to have a sister like Andrea."

Do this with every child individually. Don't be afraid to repeat the process every now and then. You will find the results to be absolutely joyful!

Dear Larry:

Holidays are a nightmare at our house. We have four children; two from my previous marriage and two from my husband's. Mine live with us full-time, and his live across town but spend every other weekend with us. They are all between the ages of ten and fourteen.

Here's the problem. Everyone fights over where the kids are going to spend the holidays. Even the grandparents put in their two cents' worth. When agreements are finally made between the adults, then the kids start refusing to go along with the plans.

It's a mess. Lots of tears, lots of screaming matches, and you can cut the tension with a knife. While I don't think there is any viable solution, I thought I would ask.

—In Dread of Holidays

Dear In Dread:

It sounds as though you are experiencing the complexities of holiday planning that so many stepfamilies face. Whenever you have so many people to please, someone is not going to be

happy with the outcome, and everyone is likely to apply whatever pressure they can in order to swing things their own way.

There are two things you and your husband can do that will relieve the tension and stress. First, agree that the two of you will keep your cool. This is very important. If you can do it, you will have a much better chance of helping everyone else to keep his or her cool, too.

Second, spend some time asking each of the children what their preferences are. Make sure that you also ask them why they would like it to be that way. Assure each child that you will take their wishes into account when you make your final decisions. By doing so, even if you need to make a decision contrary to the children's, you will find that they will be more understanding because you took the time and effort to understand their desires.

Keeping a positive, upbeat attitude can help immeasurably as well. Good luck.

Dear Larry:

My daughter has been invited out to the prom. We trust her, but we are very concerned about her plans to go to a party at a local hotel, followed by a four A.M. breakfast. Basically, she will be out all night!

Call me old-fashioned (as my daughter does), but I just don't think this is proper. In fact, I think it is absolutely ridiculous. But my husband says, "What's the harm?" He says that's just the way things are done now and that we should let her go. What do you think?

—*Old-Fashioned Mom*

Dear Mom:

Your husband is right; that is how they do things now. But I agree with you. Personally I think a one A.M. curfew is in order. The big advantages to this tack are 1) your daughter will be under less pressure to do something she knows she shouldn't do; 2) her date will get the message that you are strict and he will behave better; and 3) you will get to bed a heck of a lot earlier!

Sure, your daughter will complain like crazy now, but she'll likely thank you in the years ahead for being strict.

Take lots of pictures and tell them to have a great time.

Dear Larry:
Our children are literally driving my husband and me to distraction. We have two sons, ages ten and eleven. They are constantly at each other's throats. They fight verbally and physically from the time they get up in the morning until they go to bed at night. Sometimes the fighting is so bad that I'm afraid someone will get badly hurt.

While I really don't think there are any viable solutions (we've tried everything), a friend of mine suggested that I write to you. So I have, and I am willing to try anything you might suggest that would help. But hurry, I'm sinking fast.

—Signed Me, a Mother on the Road to Insanity

Dear Mom:
If you follow the guidelines below, I believe the fighting and bickering in your home will diminish significantly, if not altogether.

Good communication is the basis of a strong parent-child relationship. Children who learn to identify and talk out their feelings tend to talk out their negative feelings rather than acting them out, be more autonomous and able to resist negative peer pressure, have more empathy for others, make better moral choices, and be more willing to take direction from their parents. All of these are good reasons to take the time and effort to establish a strong pattern of communication between you and your children.

To do so, follow these steps.

1. Pick a place in the house where you can sit and talk with your children without the disruption of television or radios. Identify it to your children as your talking place.
2. Spend five minutes there each day with each child, one at a time.

3. Make good eye contact.

4. Physically touch your child as he or she is talking.

5. Refrain from giving brilliant advice (the more brilliant it is, the less likely your child will follow it).

6. Ask open-ended questions like
   - What was the best part of your day?
   - What was the worst thing that happened to you today?
   - What worries you the most?
   - What are you most afraid of?
   - What do you think would make someone do something like that?
   - What don't you know?
   - What do you mean when you say . . . ?
   - What do you think you are going to do about that?

7. Practice reflective listening. Rephrase what your child is saying and repeat it back. For example, "You saw some kids fight today, is that right? How did that make you feel?"

8. Name your child's feelings and verify them; for example, "You seem real sad about what happened today, is that right?"

9. When talking with a child about what happened in a certain situation, ask "how," "what," and "when" questions, rather than "who" or "why."

10. Do not rescue your child from silence. After you ask a child a question, be silent. When you think you have been silent long enough, be silent some more.

11. Refrain from trying to talk your child out of feeling a certain way. For example, do not say, "There are no monsters or ghosts in your room. There is no reason to be afraid." Doing this causes a child to hang on more tightly to the feeling. Rather, say, "You're afraid because you think there might be ghosts and monsters in your room, is that right?" Given an opportunity to talk about it, the child can release the feeling (and learns that it is okay to talk out, rather than act out, negative feelings).

12. On occasion, say to your child, "You are really good at talking things out. I enjoy talking to you." Or put the same message in a note to your child.

Practice the above for thirty days. Once you establish it as a habit, you will never stop. Your kids won't let you! They will absolutely love it, and so will you. It will become the highlight of your day.

In addition, if you sit down with each of your children individually for five minutes each day and give them your undivided attention, I promise you that you will have children who will grow up well-adjusted and who will strive to emulate every good moral and value you emphasize to them. That is the power of the human need to have someone to listen to and understand you. Good luck!

Dear Larry,

I have low self-esteem, and so does my eleven-year-old son. I suppose he gets some of it from me, but his self-esteem gets trampled on a lot at school as well. The big problem is that he has terrible beliefs about himself. He thinks he is stupid and that nobody likes him. Of course, I tell him these things aren't true, but he won't listen to me or to his father, for that matter. Is there anything we can do to help him? I'm afraid if we don't do something, he will turn into a recluse and want to live with us forever.

—*A Concerned Mother*

Dear Concerned:

One of the most common conditions among children today is low self-esteem. What this means is that there are a lot of kids who have negative beliefs about themselves. This is too bad, because negative beliefs cause people to make decisions that are unnecessarily limiting and self-perpetuating.

What happens is this. Let's say a child picks up a belief that he isn't liked by his peers. Because human beings act according to their beliefs, this belief becomes both limiting and self-perpetuating. It is limiting because, based on this belief, the child will likely turn down opportunities to be involved in sports, service clubs, and other school activities. Every time the child decides not to participate because he believes he is not likable, he reinforces and perpetuates the belief. After a while, the belief becomes deeply ingrained, so much so that we have a term for the condition. We say the person has a "solid belief."

These beliefs are very difficult for parents to change, and they are very frustrating for parents to deal with. But there is hope and there are a few things you can do. First, insist that your son become involved in at least one sport and one youth group or service club. For the sport, you may want to consider one of the martial arts. There is a documented rise in self-esteem among children involved in learning the art of self-defense. For the youth group, both school and churches offer opportunities that will benefit your son. The more he is involved with his peers in activities that benefit other people, the better his chances of developing positive beliefs about himself.

Second, praise your child every day, and do so in this way. Look for even a small bit of concrete evidence of a positive quality, point it out, and label your child with the quality. For example, say something like "You got an A on your essay. Good job. You are good at writing." Or "You took out the garbage without being told. You are considerate and I really appreciate it."

Remember to point out something positive every day. Make sure you attach it to some bit of evidence and label your child with a positive quality. Very important, disregard any negative comments he makes about your praise. Keep on doing it every day in spite of what he says. Also make sure he participates in the sports and youth groups in spite of his complaints.

The payoff of taking the time and effort to do these things will be in having a child who will one day say to you, "Mom, you have no idea how wonderful it was to grow up having you behind me every day. I will always love you for it, and you can be assured I will do the same for my children."

Dear Larry:
Our three-year-old daughter is driving us crazy. She whines constantly, hits her brothers constantly, and won't sleep in her own

bed. She always ends up in bed with us one way or the other. Do you have any suggestions?

—A Tired Mom and Dad

Dear Tired:

Don't poop out yet. Your daughter has about one more year before she reaches what I call the "age of reason." At the age of four, children are much easier to talk to and reason with. Until then, ignore the whining, do not let her have her way when she whines. (Every time you do so, she will whine nineteen more times!) Instead, walk away from her and refuse to do what she wants.

Tell your daughter that every time she hits someone, you are immediately going to put her in her room. When she does hit, immediately put her in her room. Do not warn her, just do it. Admonish her sternly with, "No hitting." Use only these words; say them loudly and sternly, without screaming. Ignore her if she cries. Three to five minutes in time-out or until she calms down should be sufficient to get her attention.

Last, you are in charge of who sleeps where. So take charge. Refuse to let your child sleep with you. Be kind about it, but be firm. Tell her, "Sleeping in Mommy and Daddy's bed is not allowed." Keep putting her back in her own bed until she learns that you mean business. This could take as many as fourteen nights, but once you have broken her of the habit of sleeping with you, she most likely won't come back again. If you have to, lock your door so she can't climb in while you are sleeping. In sum, you're bigger than she is, so *take charge*! Good luck.

Dear Larry:

I'm embarrassed to say it, but my sixteen-year-old daughter has an awful mouth. Whenever she doesn't get her way, she screams things like "I hate you," "I don't love you anymore," and "You're stupid!" If I say anything back at her, her language just gets uglier and more defiant. If I could, I would send her away to a boarding school, but I can't afford it. Any suggestions? I'm a single mom and get no help from her father.

—An Exasperated Mom

Dear Ex:

Mothers and daughters, and fathers and sons, commonly have very difficult relationships. Often the parents are critical and the children disrespectful. The criticism mixed with disrespect forms an explosive compound that can erupt frequently into screaming matches and noncooperation on both sides.

The only way this is going to change is for you to change the way in which you relate to your daughter. Only when you change will she change. You make a pledge to immediately stop criticizing your daughter (every parent does so, so 'fess up and do what it takes to cut it out!).

Next, point out at least one thing about your daughter each day that is positive. By proving that you notice her positive qualities, you will enhance those qualities in her as well as in yourself. They don't have to be big compliments. Just small things are fine.

By focusing on her positive traits and cutting out the criticism, you will see a dramatic change in her attitude and behavior within two weeks. I guarantee it!

Dear Larry:

Homework is the problem at our house. Every night we hassle over homework with both of our sons, ages eight and twelve. Why they don't just do it instead of procrastinating and whining about it, I'll never figure out. I would be happy if I could motivate them to do it without all the hassle.

—*A Hassled Father*

Dear Hassled:

Here are three rules to insist on that will clear up your problem. First, insist that there be a designated time for homework—the earlier the better. Second, have a designated private place for each child to do his homework. Do not allow them to do their homework in front of the television or at the dining room or kitchen table. These places invite disruptions. Instead, find a private place where each child can do his homework without disruption. Third, insist that no privileges will be granted until the homework is done and checked at least for neatness. Until it is done, have rules such as no television, no telephone, no video games, no snacks, and no going outside.

By instilling these three rules, you will get your children self-motivated to come home and get their homework done in a timely manner.

Dear Larry:

My eight-year-old son was accosted by one of his classmates on the playground today. I think he did the right thing by refusing to fight and going to tell his teacher. My husband, on the other hand, thinks differently. He thinks our son should have stood up for himself and let the other boy have it with both fists flying.

This seems rather barbaric to me, even if it is a "boy" kind of thing to do. I think a person, male or female, should use his wits to get out of having to fight and should do whatever it takes to solve conflicts peacefully. To tell you the truth, I am rather shocked at my husband's attitude to the contrary.

So what do you think?

—A Pacifist Mother

Dear P.M.:

To fight or not to fight, that is your question. And it's a good one. On the one hand, it is certainly desirable for our children to learn how to resolve conflicts without resorting to violence. On the other hand, we don't want our boys to be "sissies" or tattletales.

So what do we do? For one thing, I think we should teach all of our children how to both stand up for themselves and resolve conflicts without poking their adversary in the eye.

One way of doing this is through role modeling. You might choose to talk with your spouse about how you resolved conflicts in your personal and business life. Do this within the hearing range of your children (I personally think that the average hearing range of the average child today is three miles). You will be pleasantly surprised by how much your children will pick up on. In fact, children often benefit more from listening in on conversations than from direct discussions about a given topic.

With an eight-year-old you can also use conflicts on television programs or in stories you are reading together as jumping-off points to start conversations with your child about conflict resolution. You might ask your child what he would do if he were faced with the situation portrayed in the book or on the television program.

In all of these conversations it's useful to emphasize the importance of both standing up for yourself and resolving things peacefully. Just as important is to communicate to your child your clear expectation that he can and must resolve things without resorting to violence of any kind!

Dear Larry:

Every time my daughter doesn't get her way, she accuses me of hating her. She screams, "You hate me!" and runs to her room. I try to reassure her that I love her, but the more I do, the more she accuses me of hating her.

I love her so much, it just breaks my heart every time I hear her say it, but I don't know what to do. Everything I've done so far has just made the situation worse.

I so want my daughter to know how much I love her that I'm willing to do anything. Just point the way.

—*A Heartbroken Mother*

Dear Heart:

You don't say how old you daughter is, but it really doesn't matter, because this same accusation is commonly made by children ranging from ages two to eighteen (and up!). Like every accusation, it is made for one reason: as a way to get someone to do what the accuser wants.

What happens quite commonly in a child's life is the following. In a given situation, the child doesn't get what she has her heart set on. Feeling unloved, she blurts, "You hate me!" Shocked by this allegation, the parent responds, "No, that's not true. I love you very much! Dry your tears, honey. Here, you can have what you want."

From this moment on, the child is likely to drag out her "you don't love me" strategy every time she doesn't get her way. So powerful is this strategy that some even carry it into adulthood to get what they want.

To nip this manipulation in the bud, when your child says, "I hate you!" respond with something like "It sounds like you are very angry with me right now, is that right?" In other words, help them clarify and talk about their feelings. Your child will probably reply with something like "Yeah. I'm mad at you!" To which you can say, "Yes, I understand you are mad at me. Sometimes I get mad when I can't have what I want, too." At this point your child will likely let go of her anger and accept a compromise.

This process works like magic and leads to strong, loving relationships between parents and children. I highly recommend it.

Dear Larry:
My sixteen-year-old daughter has a mouth that just won't quit. If you looked up the definition of "back talk," you would see her picture. Her language is not only disrespectful, it often borders on being abusive.

Last week, I asked her to pick up her room before she went out with her friends. She just rolled her eyes at me and walked out the door. When I hollered at her to come back, she just kept on going. When she got back we had a screaming match that ended with both of us saying things that no mother and daughter should ever say to each other.

To complicate matters, her father (from whom I am divorced) tells her that she can come live with him anytime she likes. She throws this in my face all of the time, and I am getting sick of it.

Part of me wants to tell her to go live with him, but another part of me couldn't bear losing her. But I know that things have got to change. When it comes down to it, I got along better with my former husband than I am getting along with my daughter.

—Mother in a Quandary

Dear MQ:

There are a number of issues here to be dealt with, but first let me note that what you are going through with your daughter is unfortunately all too common. Disrespectful language and attitudes among children of all ages are at epidemic proportions in this country. The good news is that there are also many children who are perfectly polite and cooperative. Fortunately, there are some things you can do to help swing your daughter over to the polite and cooperative side.

First, make a commitment to stop talking to her in any way that might be disrespectful. Instead, become the model of kindness, compassion, and respect. Doing this alone will be a giant stride in the right direction.

Second, cut criticism out and instead make sure to sincerely compliment or praise your daughter at least once per day. Find something, no matter how small, to point out that your daughter is doing well or something that you like about her. If she responds negatively, ignore it and continue with the positive comments. Eventually you will win her over.

Third, write your daughter a letter. Tell her how much you love her. In the letter, detail at least seven things that you admire about her. Put the letter in a place where she will find it just before going to bed.

Fourth, establish a place where you can sit down and talk with your daughter each day for a few minutes. Turn off the television and let the answering machine pick up the phone. Finally, each time your daughter is disrespectful to you, keep your cool and ask her to sit down and talk with you for a minute. Tell her that you understand that she is angry and ask her to tell you what is going on with her. Listen to her with all of your heart and compassion.

Concentrate on doing these things for four weeks. Most likely you will experience a dramatic improvement in your relationship. Good luck!

Dear Larry:

My daughter is just over a year and a half old and is a biter. When she gets angry or frustrated, she bites whoever is in reach. We have done everything from spanking her to biting her back, but nothing works. Got any suggestions?

—*Mother of a Biter*

Dear MB:

Biting is a stage that some children go through. Fortunately it does not last long. Even if you do nothing, your daughter will eventually stop biting people. People's natural negative reaction to being bitten will eventually cause her to stop. Do you know any sixteen-year-olds who bite? I don't.

If, however, you are in a hurry to get her to stop, here is something that can cause her to stop biting within the next two weeks.

The next time that she bites, take her by the shoulder with one hand and get right up in her face. Look her right in the eye and apply moderate pressure to her shoulder without pinching her. Then, in a very loud, stern voice, say, *"No biting!"* Do not scream, but say it very loudly and sternly. Keep it to these two words. Then turn and walk out of the room. At this point she will be very startled and upset. When she comes to you, comfort her and compassionately repeat, "No biting."

Doing this several times should take care of the situation.

Dear Larry:

We have children ages eight, ten, and thirteen. The oldest two are well behaved, but our youngest is driving us crazy. He constantly is getting into mischief, refuses to do his chores unless we stand right over him, and taunts his older brother and sister in every way imaginable.

We are at a loss as to how to correct his behavior. We have tried time-outs, reward systems, spanking, praise, and everything else we could think of. Nothing seems to work with him. Even when we take away his privileges, as you often suggest, it doesn't faze him. He just shrugs his shoulders, says he doesn't care, and goes off to do something else.

If we are to retain our sanity, we need some practical suggestions. Any ideas?

—*Two Parents at Their Wits' Ends*

Dear Wits' Ends:

Have you tried yelling and screaming? Just kidding! Although, if you are like most parents, you are at the point where you yell and scream a lot, also to no avail.

The only thing I know of that works consistently with children is to write down the rules and let them know what privileges they will lose if they break the rules. It is also wise to take privileges away for no more than a week at a time.

Of course, once your child misbehaves, you must follow through and take away the privileges for a prescribed period of time. If, as many children do, your child responds with, "I don't care," do not be disturbed. This is a common manipulation that children use very effectively against parents. What normally happens when a child says, "I don't care," is that the parent says, "I give up!" This leaves the child to go on about his merry way unobstructed.

A better parental response is to say something like "Caring is not a requirement. The only thing that is required is that you follow the rules. If you don't, you will lose your privileges." Letting your child know that you don't care that he doesn't care will defuse the power of this manipulation and should result in better behavior.

One caution here. With some children this process takes a while to work. What this means is that you have to keep it up even when it seems not to be working. This is difficult but necessary if you are to "keep your wits about you."

Dear Larry:

Our five-year-old is still sucking his thumb. Since nothing we have tried has worked to get him to stop, my husband now thinks that we should punish him every time we catch him doing it. I'm not so sure. What do you think?

—*Mother of a Persistent Thumb Sucker*

Dear Mom:

I think you are right. Punishment probably won't work. At best it may cause your son to do a better job of hiding his thumb sucking. At worst, punishment will prolong the habit.

What gets consistent results is taking your child to your dentist just before he turns six and asking your dentist to have a private talk with your child about why he should quit sucking his thumb. Sometimes having a professional person talk with your child can work like magic, even though he or she is likely to give your child the same information you have been giving him. I think it's the age-old phenomenon of kids being more likely to listen to an outside authority than to their parents. Why this is so, I don't know.

If this does not work, ask your dentist about a thumb-sucking appliance. With one of these fitted in your child's mouth, it is virtually impossible for your child to suck his thumb.

Either way will get the job done. Good luck to you and to your son (I quit smoking eight years ago and I know how difficult it is to break a habit where you stick something in your mouth and suck on it all day long).

Dear Larry:

I wonder if there's any hope for me and my son. He's nearly thirteen and is half the time in the care of a verbally abusive father whom he adores (and copies). Won't my attempts to discipline him make him more resentful? Thanks.

—*BJ in Norway*

Dear BJ:

It sounds as though you have a major challenge on your hands, and one that you have to handle on your own. When it comes down to it, though, almost every thirteen-year-old on the face of the earth is a major challenge.

If your son is like most, he will likely resent any initial attempts that you make to discipline him. However, he will get over it. In the long run, the two of you will have a much better relationship if you are a kind but firm authoritative figure in his life.

Many single mothers make the big mistake of holding back on discipline. Those who make this mistake typically end up with out-of-control, disrespectful teenagers. This is far more difficult to live with than a teen who is screaming that you are "unfair" and who threatens to go live with his father.

Dear Larry:

I have a nine- and eleven-year-old who are saying that they will not wear uniforms to school this coming year (their school voted them in for the first time). They say lots of kids are going to wear regular clothes and that they will not be one of the "dorks" to show up in a uniform.

Personally, I'm in favor of the uniforms. It will save all kinds of hassles and tears in the mornings over what to wear, not to mention the arguments at the mall over what to buy for school clothes (what a nightmare!).

But, then, I see their point, too. If their friends aren't going to wear uniforms, why would they want to show up to school dressed differently from their friends? What do you think?

—*On-the-Fence Mom*

Dear On-the-Fence:

Hmmm. Let me see now. Part of me, like you, would want to say, "I understand exactly how you feel. I wouldn't want to show up to school dressed differently from my friends, either."

Another part of me smells a rat. Whenever my kids used the argument that "all of their friends are doing it," I knew I had better dig deeper for more information. This argument often was a signal that all of their friends were telling their parents the same thing in order to "divide and conquer" the parents, and, of course, get their own way.

So, here is what I would suggest. Show them that you have some empathy for their plight and tell them you will look into it. Tell them that you will call the school and their friends' parents to see what everyone else is doing. Interject a little humor here by noting that you sure wouldn't want them to face the embarrassment of being the only kids without uniforms.

Then follow through. Find out what the new school policy says in regard to uniforms. If it is like many schools, it will say that all students must wear uniforms and that they will be sent home if dressed in street clothes. This, of course, solves the dilemma.

If, on the other hand, the policy says uniforms are optional, you will have to make your decision on what to do. In this case, call the parents of your children's friends. Find out what they are doing. If indeed they are going with regular clothes, you may want to consider doing the same. It probably wouldn't be worth all the flak you would get from your children if you made them wear the uniforms.

Have a great school year, and make sure to point out something good about your child each day. The benefits will be huge to them and to you!

Dear Larry:

My twelve-year-old daughter has become a recluse. All she wants to do is to stay in her room and read. This probably wouldn't be too bad, but she insists on reading romance novels. She gets the books from her friends and devours one a day.

The real problem is that she won't do anything else. Getting her to help around the house is impossible. Even getting her to come to dinner and eat with the family is a fight. If we can get her out of her room, she keeps her nose stuck in a book.

What should we do?

—Mom of a Preteen

Dear Mom:

Sounds like you have a very typical twelve-year-old daughter. If you do nothing, this phase will probably pass on its own. And it is a "phase." Totally normal and nothing to worry about.

Still, that doesn't mean that it isn't a good idea to set some guidelines. Living with a daughter's antisocial behavior can be a real pain. You might want to consider some rules like 1) No reading at the dinner table; 2) You must do your chores before going to your room to read; and 3) Homework must be done before pleasure reading.

At the same time, be nice to her. Too many parents make the big mistake of criticizing the heck out of their preteens when they act in aggravating ways. This serves only to damage both the self-esteem of the child *and* the parent-child relationship. The wise parent holds back the criticism and focuses on the positive instead.

Dear Larry:

My fourteen-year-old daughter is becoming increasingly resistant to going on family outings. Even when we go away for the weekend to visit relatives, she complains bitterly about having to go along. She says she hates going, that it's boring, and that she wants to be with her friends.

We are considering letting her stay with friends at least some of the time. What do you think?

Mother of a Challenging Teen

Dear Teen-Challenged Mother:

Let me be frank. Before you even leave town, your daughter and her friends will likely plan the biggest party of their lives at your house, to begin the moment you exit the city limits.

How do I know this? Well, it's just that this is what almost every self-respecting teenager does when they have access to their parents' house while their parents are out of town.

If they don't do the party thing, you can be assured that some other plans will be made to do some other forbidden and unwise fun activity in your absence. You might be saying, "Well, you don't know my daughter. My daughter wouldn't do those things."

Odds are, though, I'm right. Even really, really "good" kids do all kinds of things they shouldn't do when they are out of their parents' sphere of control, often with disastrous results.

While I understand that we must at some time leave our children unsupervised and trust that they will keep themselves out of trouble, fourteen is not the age to do it. In fact, I would postpone having to do this as long as possible, despite the constant complaining. When it comes down to it, I'd much rather put up with the arguing than come home to a child in trouble.

If you tell your children that their presence is required on family outings and visits, your children will likely curtail their complaining when they see that it's not doing any good. If not, let them take a friend along, if possible.

Dear Larry:

My mother-in-law insists on keeping up the Santa Claus thing with our five- and seven-year-old sons. We have nothing against our children enjoying the myth of Santa Claus. But that is what it is: just a story. Santa is a mythical storybook figure, and we have always presented Santa to our children this way. We think this is a healthier viewpoint. However, my mother-in-law doesn't agree, and she acts and talks as though Santa is real in front of my kids, despite knowing I don't like it.

How can I get her to stop undermining me?

—*Frustrated Daughter-in-Law*

Dear Frustrated:

I'm wondering if your mother-in-law undermines you with your children in other ways as well. If so, you have a different problem than if she opposes you only on the Santa Claus issue.

If Santa is the only issue, count your lucky stars. This will pass and is a minor issue if you get along well otherwise. I don't know of any child who has ever been psychologically warped by believing in Santa. And if your children are typical, if you don't make a big issue out of it, they won't miss a beat over the disparity between what you tell them and what their grandmother tells them. The will probably humor both of you and believe whatever their friends believe.

However, if she opposes you on a number of other issues as well, you have a much larger problem, and you are going to have to come to terms with your mother-in-law. To do this, you will need to open up a dialogue with her. This may be difficult, but you have to find some way to communicate your need for her to support you rather than undermine you.

If you can, take her to lunch, be nice (sugar catches more flies than vinegar), and explain to her that you want the two of you to present a united front to the children. It's to be hoped that she will get the message and see the virtue of joining your team for the sake of her grandchildren.

Dear Larry:

My twelve-year-old daughter tells me that she absolutely does not want to go to Michigan this year over Christmas to visit her father. The only reason she will give is that she wants to stay with her friends over Christmas vacation. She is adamant that she doesn't want to go, even to the point of saying she will refuse to get on the airplane.

I don't know what to do. My ex-husband has the legal visitation rights every other Christmas. When I try to discuss the issue with him, he is totally unreasonable. He says that I'd better put her on the plane or he will have me in court for contempt. At the same time, he says he will petition to reduce the child support.

In a way, I agree with him. I mean, I agreed to the terms of the visitation rights and child support. He has always kept his side of the bargain. And I know he has been nothing less than a great father to our daughter. But still, I want my daughter to be happy and I don't want to force her to do anything against her will. Any ideas?

—In a Dilemma

Dear Dilemma:

Golly, what a mess. Or, at least, a potential for a big mess. Someone is going to have to give in or at least compromise. Perhaps your daughter could go for several days instead of for the whole vacation. Or maybe your daughter could arrange to visit her father on a different holiday. In either case, I would make it clear to both your daughter and your ex-husband that this is an issue for the two of them to work out together. Let them know that while you want out of the middle, you are supportive of their relationship and will support any solution they come up with.

If they can't work it out, take notes. If you end up in court, you will want to be able to tell the judge exactly what happened. Chances are, though, if you stay calm and supportive of both sides, it will not end up in court.

No matter what your daughter works out with her father, be supportive of her. When it comes down to it, she is your primary concern. Your ex-husband is an adult, and he can take care of his own emotions.

Dear Larry:

I have a four-year-old son that I need help with. He whines about eeeeeverything! The milk isn't white enough, the sky isn't blue enough, and the water isn't wet enough. The list just keeps going on.

How do I break this behavior without going crazy?

—About to Be Whined to Tears in Virginia Beach

Dear Whined to Tears:

Aren't kids wonderful? They provide us with so many opportunities to practice our self-control!

Here are a couple of things that help parents extinguish or at least reduce whining. First, sit down with your son and have a talk about whining. Explain to him the difference between whining and asking for what he wants in his "grown-up" voice. Make it fun and role-play with him. Tell him that the next time he whines, you will ask him whether he wants to use his "whining voice" or his "grown-up voice." Tell him that if he chooses his whining voice, you will ask him to whine for at least one minute straight or change to his grown-up voice.

The next time he whines, in a very matter-of-fact way, ask him the aforementioned question. Most likely he will choose his grown-up voice. If not, using a watch with a second hand, say, "I see you have chosen your whining voice. I'm going to time you. Go ahead and whine for one minute. One, two, three, *go!*"

Most likely he will not be able to do it, because of what is called "paradoxical intention." That is, it is very difficult for us humans to act badly on purpose (and especially when our mother is timing us!).

If this makes sense to you, try it out a number of times (you will get better and better with practice) and let me know the outcome.

Dear Larry:

My seven-year-old son is afraid of the dark. It seems like every night he comes out of his room scared that there are monsters or ghosts in his room. We try to explain to him that there are no such things, but it doesn't do any good. What can we do to convince him?

—*An Exasperated Mom*

Dear Exasperated:

First, don't worry. This is a stage that almost all children go through. Even if you do nothing, he will outgrow these fears on his own.

Once you know this, the best tactic is to make sure that he feels that you understand his feelings and take them seriously. One of the biggest mistakes that parents make is "blowing off" their children's fears. Doing so damages the parent/child relationship and often leaves a child feeling "stupid" for feeling afraid.

Allow your son to talk about his fears. Ask him questions like "What color are your monsters? What do you think they would like to eat? Do you think they have friends? Are any of these ghosts friendly? What do you think these ghosts would say to you if they could talk?" Or simply say, "Tell me more about the ghosts and monsters in your room."

There are several advantages to allowing him to talk about his fears. First, you will be letting him know that you care about his feelings. Second, you will make him feel loved rather than stupid. Third, by allowing him to talk about his fears, you will put him in charge of them and they will dissipate much more quickly. In fact, the more he talks about his fears, the less afraid he will become.

It can also help to go to the library or bookstore with him and pick out some storybooks about children who conquered their fears.

Dear Larry:

My son is three and a half. I thought all of his "terrible twos" behavior would have subsided by now, but it hasn't. If anything, it's gotten worse. He is defiant about anything and everything, he throws tantrums every time we say no to him, and he is extremely demanding. Literally everything we have tried has failed. I try to stay calm, but most days I end up screaming my lungs out. Everyone else seems to have such nice children. I just can't figure out what we are doing wrong.

—At Wits' End

Dear Wits' End:

You have what is known as a strong-willed child. Very frustrating indeed! The good news is that there are some ways to deal successfully with such a child that will make all your lives more peaceful.

Tantrums and defiant and demanding behavior are reinforced every time you respond to them. It doesn't matter whether your response is to give in to your son or to scream and yell. Both positive and negative responses equally reinforce the unwanted behavior and increase the likelihood that it will continue.

A better strategy is to start ignoring the behavior completely. Behaviors you can ignore include crying for attention, screaming, tantrums, pouting, showing off, and arguing. Start ignoring these behaviors immediately, along with any other negative behavior that is not dangerous or damaging.

Once you start ignoring these behaviors, you must keep ignoring them. Every time you do respond, you will just reinforce the behavior, so don't allow yourself the luxury of responding. Expect that when you start ignoring these behaviors they will increase at first. But if you continue ignoring them, they will diminish markedly over a period of two to three weeks.

Next, be sure to give your son lots of praise when he is acting appropriately. The combination of ignoring negative and rewarding positive behavior virtually always works, given time and persistence.

Dear Larry:

I have a son who has a great talent for motocross racing. He has been all over the East Coast and has won about 100 races in five years. Along with the wins have come some big achievements, like finishing fifth in the nation in 2001. He also has had some of the worst luck with injuries.

This year, after winning about ten races in a row, he just decided to quit. He wasn't hurt, gave no reason, just quit. I've talked to a *lot* of fathers who also have great racers. Some of these kids have even gone pro and are on TV. They tell me that they have gone through this, but they didn't let their kids quit. They made them keep going until they were fifteen or sixteen and then gave them a choice. I must say that kids have so many things going on around them that the parents need to see their talent and help them pursue it. Tiger Woods made that same statement when he was asked about his early years. He said his father wouldn't let him quit. Look at him today. The same with Michael Jordan and others.

So, what is the right thing for me to do? Some days he says he wants to still race. Some days he's not sure. But that's all he talks about. He's eleven now and has been racing since the day he turned five. He has no other interests. Help me by giving your thoughts.

—A Father Wanting to Do the Right Thing

Dear Father:

This is an interesting issue. Solomon might even have a tough time with this one. Nevertheless, let me add my thoughts to the many I am sure you have received from others.

First, it seems to me that you have your son's best interests in mind. Otherwise you wouldn't be asking what to do. Parents who live vicariously through their children's achievements can get so obsessed with what their children are doing that they lose sight of their children's needs. This is not a good thing.

Assuming that you are not one of these parents, let me point this out. Human beings, children and adults alike, make choices based on reasons that make sense to them. They constantly assess situations and make the choices that they think will best meet their needs at the time.

This means two things in relation to your son. First, your son has a reason for wanting to quit. Second, he thinks that the decision to do so will best serve his needs. Often people don't share their true motivations for their decisions with others because they are fearful of others' responses.

Knowing this, in order to make an informed decision as a parent, you will need to sit down with your son, assure him of your love and support, and tell him that you are sure he has a good reason for wanting to quit but that you need to know what it is.

There is a good chance that your son wants to quit because of a fear of some sort. If this is the case, he might be best served by your being really positive with him and supporting him in continuing. Perhaps you can talk him into continuing for six months and then quitting if he still feels the same way (which he most likely will not).

I hope this is helpful. Please let me know the outcome.

Dear Larry:
I have an eight-year-old boy who still doesn't use the bathroom all the time. We know that he is capable of using the toilet properly. It does not bother him if he has dirty pants or wet pants. We have tried grounding, ignoring it, talking to him, but nothing seems to work. He does not have the accidents at night when he is sleeping, or at school. Most of them happen when he is at home. I know he does it partly for attention, but he says that's not it. He just doesn't care. We would appreciate any help you can offer us.

Thank you.

—Melody and Craig

Hi, Melody and Craig:
There are several common possibilities and solutions to consider. He may be soiling his pants because of a physical problem, as a means for getting attention, because of a recurring

situation that produces anxiety, or simply because he gets really involved in some activities and does not stop to use the toilet.

To rule out the physical problem, have him checked by his pediatrician. It is possible that the problem is physical and needs medical treatment. I know this because I had this problem as a child and it was purely physical. It took many trips to the doctor before they figured it out, but once they did, the problem was surgically corrected and I never had any further problem.

If it is attention-getting behavior or if he just gets so involved with playing that he forgets to go to the bathroom, then this means he has bladder and bowel control problems and needs to learn to exercise that control. To do this, set up some consequences for him. Tell him what privileges you will take away if he soils his pants. However, take the privileges away only for a week at a time and give them back each Monday.

It is also important to find out if there is something happening at school or at home that is causing him anxiety. It could be that there is another child who is bullying him, or perhaps he is intimidated by the teacher or by some recurring situation like spelling or math tests. To find out, make an appointment with his teacher and enlist her help in finding out what the problem is.

Finally, take heart. Assuming the problem is not physical, peer pressure will take care of the problem sooner or later.

Dear Larry:

Help!

I'm soon to become the stepmother of a nearly nine-year-old boy who has been spoiled, overindulged, and catered to in almost every possible way. He lies habitually, he's a thief, he's utterly defiant, he has absolutely no respect for anyone or anything, he feels no remorse, and he is an expert at manipulation and creating havoc and making the whole world revolve around him. The list could go on and on.

His mother legally turned him over to his dad, as she was at her wits' end. Currently this boy is in my total care, as his father is out of town on business. Regrettably, from what I've been told, his dad has not experienced what I've been experiencing—the unbelievable tantrums and defiance.

I have an almost one-year-old who is at the other end of the spectrum. I'm not saying he's an "angel"—he has his moments—but nothing like those of my boyfriend's son. My boyfriend is a wonderful guy, but in his relationship with his son he's more like a "buddy" than a parent. It seems to have communicated to this child that he's an adult and can call all the shots. He is in counseling, yet no one but his mother and I have experienced these unbelievable occurrences. I think it is slowly coming to Dad that he's got a monster. He's embarrassed and ashamed yet continues to make excuses for his son's behavior, blaming it on the boy's mother.

If you've got any suggested reading, I'd be grateful.

Thank you!

Dear Help:

What you describe is unfortunately very common in split families. However, show me a child who is acting out and I will show you some parents who are acting out. Children's behavior normally mirrors what is going on with their parents. Sane behavior from parents begets sane behavior from children, and vice versa.

In the same vein, I never met a child who just woke up one morning and decided to start acting out. Rather, children react to what is going on around them. So when the parents get their act together, the child will, too—and probably not before.

As to suggested reading, the bookstores are full of good books on both parenting, divorce, and stepfamilies. I, of course, recommend mine (please see Web site: www.smartdiscipline. com).

Thanks for writing.

Dear Larry:

Do you have any advice for better ways to get through the morning routines of getting dressed, brushing, hair, etc.? I have two girls—ages two and three years—and every morning is a battle.

I have tried everything I can think of, as well as the pediatrician's suggestions.

—*Jamie B.*

Dear JB:

First, do everything possible the night before to prepare for the next morning. Have clothes laid out (including yours), the breakfast table set, and do anything else you normally do in the morning but could do in advance. The less you have to do in the morning, the easier and better your morning routine will go.

Second, do whatever it takes to add happiness to your morning routine. Be enthusiastic, positive, jovial, energetic, and chipper! Leave the television off and turn on happy music. Sing and dance and humor your children as you all get ready for your day. Do this even if you don't feel like it. It is perfectly okay to fake it! By doing so, you will find that your mornings will cease to be battles. Instead they will become the delight of your day.

In sum, be proactive. Prepare the night before. Then, treat your children as the wonderful, special people that they are. Model happiness, regardless of how you are actually feeling.

Dear Larry:

Our daughter is twenty and she lives with us while she attends college. Financially this is a good arrangement, but the conflict is driving her father and me nuts. What I mean is this. At ten o'clock in the evening when we are getting ready for bed, our daughter is getting ready to go out. Most nights she comes back anywhere between two and four in the morning. This is driving us insane. When we try to talk to her about how disruptive this is to our family, she just screams at us that she is over eighteen and she can do whatever she wants.

There is just no talking to our daughter. She refuses to listen to anything we have to say. Her attitude is so bad that we are even concerned now that her nine-year-old sister is going to pick it up. We do not have a solution other than throwing her out of the house, which we are very reluctant to do. Any suggestions?

—*Parents at End of Rope*

Dear Parents:

I can just imagine many other parents reading this and saying something like "Hey, they are talking about our daughter/son." That is because the scenario you describe is a common experience in homes all across America that have eighteen-to-twenty-year-olds living in them. It is a knotty problem fraught with emotional landmines that can go off at the slightest provocation.

Here are some suggestions. When things are calm, sit down and talk with your daughter. Explain to her that while she lives in your home she will have to follow some rules. Tell her that you are willing to negotiate these rules with her, but they will have to be rules that can be lived with by everyone in the house. Then explain to her that if she is not willing to abide by the rules, she will have to live elsewhere, even if it means her having to drop out of college to support herself. Last, explain to her that you are completely serious about this.

If she believes that you are serious about making her move out, this should help motivate her to change her behavior and her attitude. If she does not believe you, she will likely keep up her antics until you finally say, "That's it. You have to move out."

Yes, I know putting a child out of the house is difficult. However, it is necessary for the child to one day be thrown out of the nest if she is ever going to learn to fly solo in life. Letting an adult child live in the comfort of the family home actually is a disservice to a child, and the longer the condition is allowed, the longer the child's personal growth is stilted.

Dear Larry:

I am appalled by the number of parents who don't keep their children in line in public places. They let them run rampant in the stores and in the restaurants. The other day I even saw a child push some books off the shelf at the library. When her mother told her to stop, she pushed some more books down. Her mother said, "That's not nice," and picked up the books while her daughter ran off and yanked a book out of another child's hands. When the mother told her to give it back, her little girl threw it at the boy and ran off!

What is the world coming to? And why can't parents seem to discipline their children anymore?

—Aggravated Mother of Well-Behaved Adult Children

Dear Aggravated:
I, too, used to get aggravated at this sort of thing. Now I just smile and decide to "be happy." I know that what I am witnessing is a young parent learning one of his or her lessons in parenting. Unfortunately, parenting is mainly an "on the job" learning experience, and these learning experiences can be painful for the child, the parent, and innocent bystanders.

The good news is that most parents do learn their lessons well and eventually get their children under control. Those who don't deserve every bit of pity they can get. There are few things in life that are worse for a parent than having a child who is totally out of control. Show me a child who is out of control and I will show you parents who are not only totally stressed out, but probably spending thousands of dollars trying to fix the situation.

Little can be done by bystanders to help the situation when a child's behavior is less than exemplary. If there is one thing that parents hate, it's interference from other people telling them how to raise or discipline their children. Don't do it even if it is easy to spot the parents' folly. Let the parent learn his or her own lessons, hard as they may be.

The one big exception to this is child abuse. If you witness a child being physically abused, then by all means report it to the police. To do so, you may have to overcome your own reticence to "get involved" or your propensity to "mind your own business." Remember that child abuse, left unchecked, gets worse over time, not better. This child's only chance of being rescued may be for you to speak out.

Dear Larry:
I need help with my ten-year-old boy, James. He has a hard time in school (academically and socially). He doesn't pay attention to what the teacher says, he's very easily distracted, and he shows no sign of enthusiasm toward school.

At home, James always has a hard time following instructions, especially when it is something that doesn't interest him. He talks back more and more to me and shows signs of disrespect.

What can I do? His self-esteem is going down the drain. I know there are many things that I didn't do well with him, but I don't want him to be angry, feel that he is stupid, and have an unhappy life. Please help me.

—*Mother of James*

Dear Mother of James:
Thanks for writing. It sounds as if you have a number of legitimate concerns about your son. It is wise to do something now, because once your son enters into the teen years, change will be much more difficult.

The best way I know to get a child interested in school is to get him involved with some school-related activities, be it sports or some sort of club. Doing so will also help his self-esteem. If he is reluctant—as many kids are—insist that he participate anyway. Once he gets started he may well jump in and really love it. Also, visit the school counselor and ask for his or her guidance. Often the counselor can help set up other avenues of help for both parents and students.

Dear Larry:
How about an eight-year-old daughter that just can't (or won't) keep her room straightened up? I think she is old enough to put her clean clothes away, but she doesn't, so I do. I am *not* "Martha Stewart," but I do like my house in order!
Thank you!!

—*Not the Maid, Either*

Dear Not Either,
Make a rule that her room must be picked up and chores completed before privileges can be enjoyed. In other words, no television, no phone, no going outside, no playing, no computer, and no games until her work is done. I believe children should have

chores and various responsibilities. Children whose parents insist that they participate in meaningful household duties have higher self-esteem and self-confidence than those whose parents take care of all the important stuff.

Dear Larry:

We have a question about our seven-year-old daughter. She is very hard to get moving on some mornings, not all mornings. We also have trouble getting her motivated to get ready for other activities such as soccer practice. We have taken away activities, TV, and several other items, but we haven't found the right method yet. We would love to hear any other suggestion.

—*Resolute Parents*

Dear Parents,

Some children are tougher to get going in the mornings than others. Here are three suggestions. Help her get ready for the next morning the night before. Pick out clothes, get schoolbooks ready, and take care of anything else that will make the morning go smoother. Next, eliminate morning television. Make it taboo. Third, if she still dilly-dallies in the morning, give her a deadline to be ready each morning. Tell her if she misses her deadline, then she will not have any privileges that evening. Also, tell her that you are not going to prod her or remind her. Rather, it is totally up to her to decide whether or not she wants to meet the deadline and to have her privileges.

As for the soccer practice, tell her you will take her whenever she is ready. Whether she gets into trouble with the coach or not is between her and her coach.

Dear Larry:

Our daughter, Amy, is five years old, in kindergarten at a Montessori school. We are pleased with the progress she has made in doing what she knows needs to be done, *when* it needs to be done. A problem we are having now is with Amy not telling the truth. I realize that she is at the age where fantasy can get confused with reality. Sometimes she will claim with great

sincerity that she has washed her hands before the meal, brushed her teeth after a meal, etc., and when pressed, will admit that she in fact had not. She usually does these tasks by herself. She knows to ask (and often does) if she needs help.

We will occasionally watch to confirm that she is doing them properly. Do you have any thoughts or suggestions to share with us?

Thanks.

—Charlie S.

Dear Charlie:

Sounds to me like you are doing just fine. And you are correct. All children go through this phase. They are testing out the phenomenon of lying. All you really need to do is what you are already doing. Let her know that lying is not allowed in your family and that if she lies, she will be punished. One caution, though. Many parents fall into the trap of thinking they need proof of the lie. You don't. Proof is for courts. Parents need only exercise their best judgment. If you think she is lying, she probably is.

Also, don't fall into the trap of trying to get her to admit to something you already know she did. Simply confront her with it and act accordingly. If she tries to lie about it, matter-of-factly remind her that in your family lying is not allowed.

Dear Larry:

I'm having problems in the way my new husband wants to discipline the kids. Both of them are ADHD and have some behavior problems. They aren't bad kids. He doesn't want to interact with them at all, even when they are well behaved. He says he married me and not the children; however, before we married, he said he would love them as his own.

We cannot seem to agree on any discipline issues. When they do misbehave he shuns them, and when they do behave he says they should always behave. I don't know what to do at this point or where to go. Neither of us has much faith in counseling. What direction do you suggest we take on solving this issue?

—A Disappointed New Bride

Dear New Bride:

I have given your question a good deal of thought. Stepparenting, as you well know, is very difficult. But the key word is "parenting." In order to have a successful, happy family, both parents must participate actively in raising the children, and part of this involves disciplining them. The consequence of only one parent in a stepfamily participating in parenting can be dire. Most couples in remarriages divorce. Currently 70 percent of remarriages fail. When asked why, most say it was because of the children.

This is not to say that it is the children's fault. The divorces take place rather because the parents were unable to resolve the issues surrounding the children. These issues are often difficult, complex, and emotionally charged. Handling them without any outside help is often difficult, if not impossible.

Given this, I have three suggestions for you to consider. First, I would suggest you purchase a book or two on stepfamilies. Knowledge can go a long way toward helping you resolve your problems. Second, I would call your local parenting center and ask if it offers any courses or support groups for stepparents. Most do, and being in a program with others facing the same problems you are can be very helpful.

Third, although you do not have a lot of faith in counseling, you may need some. Therefore start asking around (friends, doctor, minister) about which therapists are really good at helping stepparents. Find out which ones get good results, call them, and discuss your situation with them. If you find someone you feel you could relate to and who you think might be able to help you, make an appointment and go see him or her. If your husband refuses to go, go alone.

One more thing. It sounds as if your husband is reacting emotionally to the situation. Perhaps there is some anger or fear that he needs to talk with you about, and a listening ear on your part could help the situation.

I hope some of this is helpful to you.

Dear Larry:

My three-year-old son was invited to a birthday party at Chuck E. Cheese (a child-friendly pizza place he adores—we play

there for hours). However, for the past month, we have been working with our son to 1) sleep in his own bed (all night); 2) get dressed for day care in the morning without much complaint; and 3) brush his teeth without whining.

When he does these things (or exhibits other exceptionally nice behavior), we reward him with a Batman sticker for his sticker chart (hangs outside his bedroom). And we've promised him that when all the blanks on his sticker chart are filled, (there are a hundred of 'em, and he achieves anywhere from one to four stickers per day), we will take him to Chuck E. Cheese. This sticker program worked great when we were potty training him because he loves Chuck E. Cheese (he was so proud of himself when that chart was full and to this day rarely has "accidents").

The point is this. I don't believe I should let him attend this birthday party because he's only halfway through his sticker chart, and I don't want to confuse him with taking him to Chuck E. Cheese before his chart is full. Am I being too strict? He doesn't even know he's invited to the birthday party. I'm afraid I'll send him mixed messages if we attend the party. What do you think?

—A Mom Wanting to Do the Right Thing

Dear Mom:

From your letter it is easy to tell that you are very attentive to making sure your son does well in life. This is a good thing.

Knowing that you are a wonderful mother helps me answer your question. I think you already know the answer, or you wouldn't have the insight to be asking the question.

Let him go and have a great time at the party. He will only be a child for a little while and will benefit greatly from all the fun and socialization.

As for being concerned about confusing him, don't be. Part of the learning process for a child (and parent) is to learn that there are almost always exceptions to rules. Sometimes these exceptions work for you and sometimes against you. So you might as well learn to be flexible.

In sum, go and have fun. And say hi to Chuckie for me

(after raising five children and attending a zillion birthday parties at his place, I'm sure he will remember me!).

Dear Larry:

I have to admit this, but my daughter, age five, has a best friend who drives me to distraction. The truth of the matter is that she just plain gets on my nerves.

She is completely selfish and self-centered. She hogs everything, is mean to the other kids (including my daughter), and takes pride in making other kids cry. Her manners are atrocious, and I can't see why in the world my daughter would want to be friends with her.

When I try to talk with my daughter about inviting another girl or two over to play, she insists on inviting her "best friend" instead.

I'm not only irritated, but also afraid this girl's bad traits are going to rub off on my daughter. I'm wondering if I should put my foot down and refuse to let my daughter play with this girl. Is this inadvisable?

—*Driven to Distraction*

Dear Driven:

It's just as likely that your daughter's good traits will rub off on her "best friend." Controlling your children's choice of friends is often a losing battle. They end up just going behind their parents' backs to play with them anyway.

It's far better to put your energy into getting to know this other girl and supporting the relationship. Close friendships are invaluable in a child's life and in the development process.

In order to better tolerate this girl, do two things. Sit down with both girls and explain the rules of your house and what the consequences are for breaking the rules. For example: No running in the house. If you run, I will warn you once. The next time, your playtime will be cut short.

Second, and most important, force yourself to notice a few good points about your daughter's friend. Then make a point of complimenting her at least once each time you see her.

If you do this, watch out! You will soon find yourself liking the girl!

Dear Larry:

I have a son who is going into the sixth grade this fall. This wouldn't normally concern me, but my brother's son started middle school last year and he all but flunked out. This was really a shock to the whole family, as he did just fine in grade school, both with his grades and with his behavior. In fact, he loved school. Now it's the opposite. He spends half his time in the time-out room and fights his teachers and his parents every step of the way. I know this whole thing has put my brother's family in a constant state of crisis.

My husband I want to do whatever we can to avoid this kind of thing from happening to our son. We are highly motivated to put whatever prevention measures in place that we can and we are looking for suggestions.

—*Sincerely, A Preventative Mom*

Dear Mother of Prevention:

Looking ahead to avoid problems with children is certainly a good thing. Here are a few ideas to keep in mind.

Children can be incredibly different, even in the same family. Given the exact same situation and circumstances, they can react in completely opposite ways. Some children have trouble with the transition from grade school to middle school, and some do not. So I would not lose any sleep over the situation at this point.

However, there are some things you can do that will greatly ease your child's transition into middle school. Before he starts school this fall, talk to him about the changes he is going to encounter in middle school, especially having to change classes. Let him know that this can take some getting used to and that he may encounter some problems. Tell him this is to be expected and that he will overcome them as time progresses.

Next, scout around for a good program that addresses the physical and emotional changes that come with entering adolescence. Often these programs are offered by hospital community education departments. Knowing what to expect in these areas can make all the difference to a child this age. One of the big advantages to them is that they find out that they are "normal"—a big relief to kids.

As school gets under way it is also important to insist that your child be involved in at least one or two extracurricular activities. Students who are involved in music, sports, cheerleading, church groups, scouting, and community-based clubs experience fewer problems than those who are uninvolved. Getting some children involved is no problem, as they seek out involvement on their own. Others avoid it. It is with these children that it is important to insist on involvement. Even though they may fight it, they may well thank you for your insistence once they make friends within the group.

Also, avoid the mistake that so many parents make when their children enter either middle school or high school: curtailing parental involvement with the school and the teachers. Often parents who were highly involved with their child's school during the elementary years stop going to school conferences and events because their child starts to complain. In fact, most middle school students are mortified at the thought of their friends seeing their parents. This is natural. Don't let it dissuade you. Research clearly indicates that students whose parents are involved with the school consistently do better than those students whose parents are not.

Another good idea is to have a family meeting and talk about the start of school. Decide together on changes in the family schedule that will need to take place, such as bedtimes and the time to get up. Agree on starting the new schedule enough in advance of the start of school to get used to it before the big day arrives.

At the same time, you can do yourself and your children a favor by explaining to them that from now on they will be responsible for getting themselves up and ready for school in the morning. Explain that you are resigning as their personal alarm clock and timekeeper. Let them know what consequences they will face on any given day that they fail to be ready on time.

Last, stay alert for possible problems. Make appointments to discuss any concerns you may have with your child's teachers, guidance counselor, and, if need be, school principal. Follow through on suggestions, and keep abreast of any difficulties until they are resolved. And keep an open mind to the possible needs your child may develop for additional help. These may include such things as tutoring or counseling. Either of these, for some children who have difficulty in adjusting to adolescence, can make the difference between tremendous success and protracted frustration.

Good luck and happy parenting!

INDEX